DATE			
		Y	

Jack Kerouac

Twayne's United States Authors Series

TUSAS 507

JACK KEROUAC
Coney Island, early 1950s
Photograph by John Kingsland
Courtesy of the unspeakable visions
of the individual

Jack Kerouac

By Warren French

D.H.L., Ohio University

Twayne Publishers
A Division of G.K. Hall & Co. • Boston

Jack Kerouac

Warren French

Copyright © 1986 by G.K. Hall & Co.
All Rights Reserved
Published by Twayne Publishers
A Division of G.K. Hall & Co.
70 Lincoln Street
Boston, Massachusetts   02111

Copyediting supervised by Lewis DeSimone
Book production by Elizabeth Todesco
Book design by Barbara Anderson

Typeset in 11 pt. Garamond
by P&M Typesetting, Inc., Waterbury, Connecticut

Printed on permanent/durable acid-free paper
and bound in the United States of America

Library of Congress Cataloging in Publication Data

French, Warren G., 1922–
  Jack Kerouac.

  (Twayne's United States authors series; TUSAS 507)
  Bibliography: p. 135
  Includes index.
  1. Kerouac, Jack, 1922–1969—Criticism and interpretation.   2. Bohemianism
in literature.   3. Bohemianism—United States.   I. Title.   II. Series.
PS3521.E735Z6328   1986   813'.54   86-4817
ISBN 0-8057-7467-X

*For Bob DeMott, Carol Harter,
Dean McWilliams, Jim Thompson,
and my other friends of the
English faculty at Ohio University;
for Ken and Tom,
who first brought me to Athens;
and for Minghan Xiao and Scott Miner
and the other members of the seminar
who helped me get this book on the road.*

Contents

About the Author

Warren French was born only a few weeks before Jean-Louis Kerouac in another decaying East Coast industrial port, Philadelphia, where he grew up and attended (like Kerouac's fictional alter ego in *The Town and the City*) the University of Pennsylvania. After serving in the U.S. Army from Austria to the Philippines during World War II, he earned his graduate degrees at the University of Texas-Austin and began his four decades of college teaching at the University of Mississippi while William Faulkner was still resident in Oxford.

Since then he has taught at the University of Kentucky, Stetson University, the University of Florida, Kansas State University, and the University of Missouri-Kansas City. Since 1970 he has been on the faculty of Indiana University-Purdue University at Indianapolis, from which he retires in May 1986 to devote himself to writing and promoting American Studies abroad. He has received the honorary degree of Doctor of Humane Letters from Ohio University.

Warren French has been associated with Twayne's United States Authors Series since its inception, contributing early volumes on John Steinbeck, Frank Norris, and J. D. Salinger. He has edited the titles on contemporary American literature since 1977, as well as all the volumes in Twayne's Filmmakers Series. He has also published *The Social Novel at the End of an Era,* edited a series of volumes of original essays on the American literature of the decades from the 1920s to the 1950s, *American Winners of the Nobel Literary Prize* (with Walter Kidd), and *The South in Film.* He has served on the editorial boards of *American Literature, Western American Literature, Twentieth Century Literature, American Studies, The Journal of American Studies,* and the *Literature/Film Quarterly.* Following his retirement, he plans to spend most of his time on the road abroad, operating from a home base by the sea in Swansea, South Wales.

Preface

For a long time I have had a special interest in Jack Kerouac, because he has seemed to me to resemble in many ways both John Steinbeck and J. D. Salinger, about whom I wrote some of the earliest books published in this series. All three had published in their thirties novels that have become midcentury classics and then had failed to follow up on their triumphs. Each had become upset about the celebrity his work had won him and begun to withdraw from public view, leaving his audience behind in pursuit of private goals that attracted increasingly adverse criticism. When the contract for a long-projected book about Kerouac for this series was vacated, I appealed to take over the assignment myself in order to complete not something with the tight unity of a trilogy, but a kind of verbal triptych.

I have been particularly interested in Jack Kerouac because he and I are such close contemporaries. He was born in Lowell, Massachusetts, only a few weeks after my own birth on 26 January 1922 in another declining East Coast industrial city, Philadelphia. The difference in my being a visionary Aquarian rather than a slippery and sad Pisces could account for different worldviews despite similar temporal experiences. Like Kerouac's, my impressionable years were passed during the demoralizing Depression. We both discovered our quite different identities and were set on the courses that would shape our careers in 1935 at the age of thirteen; and we both ended up—for quite different tenures—at Ivy League universities (from the stands I may even have seen him on the bench during a Penn-Columbia football game). When *On the Road* was at last published, I was the counselor of the Beatcult students at the University of Florida, who hung out at the coffee houses that flourished then even there. Our paths split in 1960, when we both made our trips into the valley. Kerouac's led to Florida and early death in St. Petersburg; mine led out of Florida and at last to a new life in the old world where he had never been able to feel at home. Functioning as an English Department head in Kansas City during the late 1960s, while Kerouac became increasingly alienated from the activist generation he had helped spawn, I identified the door to my inner sanctum with one of his most Beat photographs,[1] which I took down forever in October 1969.

So much has already been written about Kerouac, especially so many biographies prompted by and encouraging a greater interest in his life than his work, that I felt at a loss for a while about how to justify yet another eavesdropping on a writer who was enjoying a revival as a cult hero. Then while I was editing one of Jerome Klinkowitz's brilliant reviews of current criticism of contemporary fiction for *American Literary Scholarship 1983,* I was struck by his statement on the shortcomings of recent appraisals of Kerouac: "How Kerouac's own life resisted his attempts at literary legendizing still demands more investigation."

I have set out, therefore, to respond to Klinkowitz's challenge, to try to offer hypotheses about Kerouac's failure, despite his grandiose ambitions, to forge from the materials of his own experience a transcendent Jack Duluoz, the kind of legendary figure that James Joyce, whom Kerouac greatly admired and tried to emulate, made of Stephen Dedalus.

It must first be said that to a certain extent Kerouac did succeed. He did produce a series of related novels, based upon but not slavishly chronicling his own life. These he collectively called "The Duluoz Legend." But he did not live to coordinate these as he talked of doing, and he left important gaps in the narrative. Klinkowitz's judgment, moreover, that this effort failed to achieve truly legendary stature is irrefutable. Kerouac's most famous and best selling work, *On the Road,* which has become a legend, is not really a part of the final form of the Duluoz Legend. It was only a stage in Kerouac's search to find the appropriate form for legendizing a particular phase of his life. It was superseded by *Visions of Cody,* which remains little read, though highly praised by some admirers of Kerouac's stylistic experiments. *On the Road* is, furthermore, very probably the most heavily edited of Kerouac's works, so that the text that won him a celebrity that he came to detest and fear is probably the least representative expression of his vision.

For various reasons, what I consider the unmistakable segments of the Duluoz Legend have never attracted the following that *On the Road* has, so that Kerouac's effort to create a legend generally proved a failure, even though it reaches a powerful conclusion in *Big Sur,* Kerouac's—and possibly his era's—most undervalued novel. What happened? I shall try to suggest an answer to this question by presenting a reading of Kerouac's work organized in a fashion that, despite its seemingly tempting prospects for the critic, I have not seen attempted before.

Since there are already a number of adequate biographies of Jack Kerouac, I have kept the account of his own life as brief as possible, relating only those details essential to understanding the principal events drawn upon in the Duluoz Legend and avoiding especially the fund of anecdotes concerning his erratic behavior during his last sad years that has grown into a kind of mean-spirited legend of its own.

The larger part of this book is devoted instead to a reading of the works constituting the Duluoz Legend, not in the order in which they were written or published, but, as nearly as possible, in the chronological order of the events in Kerouac's own life upon which they were based. I begin with the stories of childhood in Lowell, *Visions of Gerard* and *Doctor Sax,* and move on to the narratives that bridge Kerouac's moves from his hometown to the city and the road, *Maggie Cassidy* and *Vanity of Duluoz.* These are followed by the books that detail the years on the road—*Visions of Cody, Tristessa, Desolation Angels,* and *Book of Dreams.* We come to the end of the road with the monumental *Big Sur* and its wispish coda, *Satori in Paris.*

Five novels sometimes included in accounts of the Duluoz Legend, even Kerouac's own enumeration of it, are omitted from this sequence and treated earlier in this book as extensions of Kerouac's life. *The Town and the City* is an apprentice work, written while he was heavily under the influence of Thomas Wolfe, that takes too many liberties with the events of Kerouac's life to be compatible with the later fictions; indeed Kerouac's last major effort was to supersede it with *Vanity of Duluoz,* an account of the same years that accords much more closely with Kerouac's life. My reservations about *On the Road* as a preliminary work that Kerouac thought he had already moved beyond have already been mentioned. The posthumous *Pic,* seemingly Kerouac's last work, proves not even a late one, but one of the discarded steps towards *Visions of Cody* that has little relationship to Kerouac's other writings. *The Subterraneans,* for complicated reasons explained in chapter 4, would need wholesale revisions to fit into the matrix provided by the Duluoz novels; like *The Dharma Bums* (also discussed in chapter 4), it is best regarded as a commercial enterprise that never received the necessary reworking to fit it into the larger pattern that the author envisioned. Although the two novels have been among Kerouac's most popular, they are also among his least representative and least impressively executed fictions.

Partly for the reasons explained above, I have devoted relatively little space to *On the Road,* which has usually dominated discussions of Kerouac's fiction. Whereas this popular novel has already been abundantly criticized, other works perhaps more central to Kerouac's literary ambitions have been neglected; and I would like to begin to restore a balance. I have not, however, merely recapitulated received opinion about *On the Road:* rather I argue that it is a far more carefully crafted work than has been recognized—perhaps Kerouac's best constructed, though the construction may not be entirely his own doing.

If I have paid less than the conventional attention to *On the Road,* I pay much more attention than usual to Kerouac's first published novel, *The Town and the City.* Despite—in fact because of—its tenuous relationship to the Duluoz Legend, this early work is far more important than has been perceived because it calls attention to a characteristic of Kerouac himself that is of primary importance in understanding his behavior and especially the fluctuations in his works and in his own attitudes.

As he himself has explained, two brothers of the large Martin family that the novel is about—Peter and Francis—are both based on Kerouac himself.[2] While dramatizations of most of his own important experiences are attributed to Peter, several are assigned to Francis. This early literary strategy reflects, I argue, a fundamental split in Kerouac's own personality that sparked a constant conflict within him—the kind of conflict that in any powerfully narcissistic personality is likely to have far more traumatic effects upon the individual than any confrontations with external forces. When then, throughout this book, I speak of the "Peter" and "Francis" aspects of Kerouac, I refer to the analyses of the complementary Martin brothers in my discussion of *The Town and the City* in chapter 2.

I have not attempted to evaluate Kerouac's poetry and nonfiction, as I wish to keep attention focused in the study on his attempts to create the Duluoz Legend. I agree with Lawrence Ferlinghetti that Kerouac "was a better novel writer than a poem writer,"[3] and others are better qualified to discuss the kinship of his verse to jazz rhythms. The important essays about his experiments with prose style have received extensive attention elsewhere.

I was inspired in a large measure to undertake this book by Tim Hunt's *Kerouac's Crooked Road,* the best scholarly effort so far to take the novelist's work seriously. Hunt has also been most helpful in sharing with me his research notes that have suggested and confirmed some of my principal observations about Kerouac's intentions. Though I have also drawn on Hunt's cogently argued theories, he is in no way responsible for my own. I could never have made the progress that I have on this book, as acknowledged in my dedication, without the aid of friends at Ohio University. Dean McWilliams was instrumental in winning me a Morton Visiting Professorship for the winter quarter 1984, during which I offered a graduate course on the Beat Generation. I am most grateful to him and the other members of the Awards Committee and the Department of English and to the administration of the university for making this productive opportunity available. My greatest impetus came from the students in the Beat Generation seminar, especially Minghan Xiao, a brilliant visitor from the People's Republic of China, who helped me see the Beat Generation afresh through the incisive questions of one becoming acquainted with it for the first time.

I also benefited greatly from a special exhibition on the work of Jack Kerouac and his associates at the Lilly Library, Indiana University-Bloomington during the summer of 1985, as well as the opportunity to use the extraordinary resources of this collection. I am also most grateful to Roy S. Simmonds for providing me with British editions and reviews of Kerouac's works and to Philip Melling for making the facilities of the Board of American Studies at the University College of Wales, Swansea, available to facilitate the completion of my work. Dave Moore, editor of *The Kerouac Connection* in Bristol has also been most helpful in acquainting me with valuable new British publications on Kerouac and in sharing material from his outstanding personal library on the Beats. Arthur and Kit Knight, masters of Kerouacana, have provided the frontispiece and much bibliographical information.

Warren French

University College of Swansea

Chronology

1922   Jean-Louis Lebris de Kerouac born on 12 March in Lowell, Massachusetts, the third child and second son of Leo Alcide and Gabrielle Ange Levesque Kerouac.

1926   Brother Gerard dies at the age of nine, on 8 July.

1933   Begins work on hand-drawn newspapers and his first novel.

1934   Observes death of the watermelon man in July.

1935   Begins his career as a football star on empty lots.

1938   Scores winning touchdown in Thanksgiving Day football game for Lowell High against archrival Lawrence High School.

1939   Graduates from Lowell High School, wins football scholarship to Columbia University, and attends Horace Mann Prep School in New York City for a year.

1940–41   Attends Columbia College.

1942   Sails to Greenland as a merchant seaman on the *S. S. Dorchester;* returns to Columbia in the fall, but quits college and football for good early in the season.

1943   Enlists in U.S. Navy, but is discharged on psychiatric grounds; sails to Liverpool as merchant seaman on *S. S. George Weems;* parents move to Ozone Park, Long Island.

1944   Meets Lucien Carr, Allen Ginsberg, and William Burroughs in June; involved in Carr's killing of David Kammerer on 14 August, but charges are eventually dropped; marries Edie Parker on 22 August and moves to Detroit, but soon separates from her.

1945   Marriage annulled; collaborates with Burroughs on an unpublished novel, "And the Hippos Were Boiled in Their Tanks."

1946   Kerouac's father dies; Kerouac meets Neal Cassady and begins work on *The Town and the City.*

1947 Makes first cross-country tour to Denver and San Francisco and back to New York.

1948 Meets John Clellon Holmes; completes *The Town and the City* and begins work on earliest version of *On the Road*.

1949 Early in the year travels with Cassady to New Orleans to visit Burroughs and later to San Francisco.

1950 *The Town and the City* published 2 March; in June drives to Mexico City with Cassady; marries Joan Haverty on 17 November.

1951 Writes third (the published) version of *On the Road* on a single roll of paper in three weeks during April and May; separates from second wife; mother moves to join sister Nin in North Carolina.

1952 Lives from January to May with the Cassadys in San Francisco; visits Burroughs in Mexico City where he writes *Doctor Sax*.

1953 Writes *The Subterraneans* in New York.

1954 Begins Buddhist studies in California and New York.

1955 Viking Press accepts *On the Road* in July; Kerouac goes to California and meets Gary Snyder; attends poetry reading at the Six Gallery in San Francisco on 13 October at which Allen Ginsberg delivers "Howl" for the first time, and hails the occasion as the start of the San Francisco Renaissance.

1956 Works as fire lookout on Desolation Mountain in Mount Baker National Forest, Washington, June to September; revisits Mexico City and returns to New York.

1957 Sails to Tangiers in February to visit Burroughs; stays until April and travels briefly in France and England; moves his mother to Berkeley in May, but they soon return to Orlando, Florida; *On the Road* published 5 September.

1958 *The Subterraneans, The Dharma Bums;* buys home for mother in Northport, Long Island; Neal Cassady sentenced to five years in San Quentin for possession of marijuana.

1959 *Doctor Sax; Mexico City Blues; Maggie Cassidy;* delivers overvoice narration for Robert Frank's film *Pull My Daisy* (based on a play by Kerouac); begins column for *Escapade* in April.

1960 *Tristessa, Lonesome Traveler;* suffers nervous breakdown in Bixby Canyon, Big Sur, on trip to California in July and August, after New York premiere of film version of *The Subterraneans.*

1961 Participates in Timothy Leary's psychedelic drug experiments in January; publishes *Book of Dreams*; visits Mexico City in summer; returns to Orlando, Florida, to write *Big Sur* in ten days.

1962 *Big Sur;* moves back to Long Island with mother in December.

1963 *Visions of Gerard.*

1964 Moves with mother to St. Petersburg, Florida, in August; sister Nin dies 19 September.

1965 *Desolation Angels;* undertakes unsuccessful trip to France to study family genealogy.

1966 *Satori in Paris;* in May moves with mother to Hyannis, Massachusetts, where she suffers a stroke; marries Stella Sampas, sister of an old friend, 19 November.

1967 Moves family back to Lowell in January.

1968 *Vanity of Duluoz;* Neal Cassady dies in Mexico on 4 February; Kerouac briefly visits Europe with old friends from Lowell in March; moves back to St. Petersburg with mother and wife in November.

1969 Dies in St. Petersburg on 21 October of internal hemorrhaging.

1971 *Pic.*

1972 *Visions of Cody.*

1973 Mother Gabrielle dies in St. Petersburg, 14 October.

1978 John Heard plays Jack Kerouac in the film version of Carolyn Cassady's *Heart Beat.*

1982   23 July–1 August, Conference at the University of Col-
       orado celebrating the twenty-fifth anniversary of the
       publication of *On the Road.*

1985   Complete text of *Old Angel Midnight* published in En-
       gland.

Part One

The Real Jean-Louis Lebris de Kerouac

Chapter One
The Road to St. Petersburg

So many pages of print have already been lavished on the unlikely life of Jack Kerouac that one is reluctant to add to the litter. Yet if we are to consider Kerouac as a case history in the problems of self-legendizing, we must begin with a summary of the raw material from which the finished goods were fashioned. One is tempted simply to reprint a six-hundred-word biographical resume that Kerouac sent Donald Allen in the fall of 1957 at the time when the long underground writer of *On the Road* was discovering the discomforts of the glaring sunlight of celebrity,[1] for it indicates what the subject himself felt should loom large in summarizing his life.

Starting Out from Lowell: Discovery of Identity, 1922–35

The two opening sentences of this biographical statement were later enlarged into the chronological opening volume of the Duluoz Legend. Kerouac's only brother, Gerard, died at nine years of age when Jack was only four. Kerouac reports that others called Gerard "a little saint," a practice that Kerouac himself was to adopt, although the question of how much he might actually have remembered from such a tender age must be considered as we later contemplate *Visions of Gerard*.

In the resumé Kerouac tells of writing his first novel in a five-cent notebook at the age of eleven. He does not mention, as some biographers do, that as a child in a French-Canadian household, he may not have spoken English until he started school and that he may have had difficulty understanding and speaking English until his college years,[2] despite his early command of an original English prose style.

This linguistic background could, paradoxically, account for Kerouac's romantic enthusiasm for American English, which, as Tom

Clark observes, he wrote with "an almost physical love";[3] his linguistic background is almost certainly responsible for a deep split in Kerouac's personality that persisted throughout his early years and that suggests the reason for his dividing himself into the complementary characters of Peter and Francis Martin in *The Town and the City* (the latter, furthermore, a twin of a brother much like Gerard Kerouac). As long as Kerouac stayed at home, his life with his family was experienced in Quebecois;[4] but upon starting to school and having to mix with children from a variety of backgrounds, he would have been forced to recognize that if he was to make a place for himself in this larger society, he must master English. Quebecois became, therefore, the language in which he expressed his deep affection for his family and treasured his earliest recollections, whereas English had to be the language of commercial success, through which he might achieve those "white ambitions" he attributes—somewhat ruefully—to Sal Paradise in *On the Road.*[5]

Kerouac's rapid development of a surprising fluency in his adopted language might have been noticed by an astute observer as one of the first evidences that the boy was marked for an extraordinary career as a manipulator of words. Stanley Aronowitz has recently questioned whether widespread functional illiteracy in the United States may not be so much a failure of the educational system as "part of a larger struggle by minority and working-class kids to hang on to their own culture and avoid deracination."[6] Such suspicions of literacy, especially in an unnatural tongue were even more rife in the 1930s than fifty years later, and even in Kerouac's childhood his way with words must have been viewed with grave suspicion by his more conventional classmates in the Roman Catholic elementary schools of Lowell's French-Canadian neighborhoods. Kerouac's infatuation with language, however, indicates that he was motivated, at least partly, by a drive to break with an inhibiting past. His interest in language was prodigious. When he was only eight he began writing "home movies" (one of these is recalled in *Doctor Sax*) and then turning them into his own comic strips. He began to compile laboriously by hand his own newspapers and magazines; and at the age of eleven he began to write his first novel about "an orphan boy running away, floating down a river on a boat," an apparently quite slavish imitation of *The Adventures of Huckleberry Finn.*[7] He then turned to writing adventure stories modeled on 1930s movies; and by the time he was fourteen he had apparently determined to become a writer, despite his family's well-grounded misgivings about the perils of such an unconventional and unpromising calling.

Meanwhile the Jesuit teachers at St. Joseph's parochial school had noticed the boy's unusual talents and quiet devotion. They induced him to serve as an altar boy and hoped that he might (like Stephen Dedalus in James Joyce's *A Portrait of the Artist as a Young Man*) develop a "vocation" for the priesthood; but any temptations he may have had to become a minister of mysteries of the church faded when he transferred in 1934 to a public junior high school.

When during his crucial thirteenth year in 1935, Jean-Louis developed a strong enough sense of his own identity to make him aggressively self-centered, the transforming experience resulted not from his precocious mind but his husky body. Kerouac was unusally set apart from his contemporaries—not just at home in Lowell—who generally regarded intelligence and athletic ability as incompatible, by being gifted both intellectually and physically (the unusual pairing provided one basis for the split self-portrait in *The Town and the City*). He had already displayed an aptitude for baseball and track, but in October 1935, he first tasted fleeting fame when he organized a sandlot football team that challenged all comers. When during the first game he scored nine touchdowns in leading his team to a 60–0 victory, he both achieved a local reputation unusual for one his age and instilled a desire for revenge into some of his affronted peers. Above all, this experience of standing out as a face in the crowd settled him on a course of trying to make his way during his teen years through his fleet-footedness on the football field.

City Lights—From the Gridiron to the Road, 1935–47

Before his finest days in football, however, young Kerouac was to have his vision darkened by some chastening experiences. One of the most frequently repeated and apparently well authenticated tales about Kerouac's youth is of his observing, as he and his mother were crossing the Moody Street Bridge over the Merrimack River in Lowell, a man carrying a watermelon collapse and die. That night he developed a fever and was "semiquarantined'" for a week until his visions of death "vanished into fantasies of life."[8]

Less easily erased were the impressions made by his first experience with natural disaster, the great flood of March 1936, when the

swollen Merrimack River put the low-lying parts of Lowell, including
father Leo Kerouac's printing plant, under water. Leo never fully recovered from this blow. Partly as a result of the expense of rebuilding
after the flood and partly as a result of his gambling, free spending,
and baiting of the political opposition, he became obliged to sell out
in order to settle his debts. After spending several cranky months at
home, he found work with a printing plant in Andover, New Hampshire, but he never regained his former position in his home commu-
nity or the pride that he had taken in it. Gabrielle had to go back to
work in a shoe factory to help make ends meet.

Undaunted, however, Jean-Louis continued his pursuit of fame at
Lowell High School. In the fall of 1937, when he was fifteen, he
never got to play on the senior football squad; but in 1938, even with
only limited opportunities, he made several spectacular touchdowns,
and it was rumored that he was being scouted by Frank Leahy, then
coach of Boston College's top-ranking football team. Then during the
traditional Thanksgiving Day game with Lowell's archrival Lawrence
High School, Kerouac broke a scoreless tie by catching a pass and
making the game's only touchdown. This triumph made him the talk
of the town and attracted recruiters from both Boston College and
Columbia University; but this early celebrity had a mixed effect upon
the impressionable young intellectual and set him on the course that
would lead him to abandon football and college and to begin a quest
for a more elusive vision. One of the most moving chapters in his first
novel, *The Town and the City,* is devoted to a description of his semi–
alter ego, Peter Martin's ambiguous feelings as he wanders about the
home town that is celebrating his performance.

Kerouac decided, however, for the time being, to stick with football. Boston College's coach Leahy, who would soon be on his way to
immortality at Notre Dame, threatened Kerouac's father, by then
back in Lowell working for an Irish family, with the loss of his job
if Jack did not sign up with the Jesuit school near Boston; but, supported by his ambitious mother, Jack opted for Columbia and New
York City. Leo did lose his job.

Jack's decision to go to New York also precipitated another crisis.
During the winter of 1939, he fell in love for the first time with an
Irish girl named Mary Carney, the model for the fictional Maggie
Cassidy. When she tried to induce him, however, to remain in Low-
ell, the affair broke up. Kerouac spent his first year in New York at
Horace Mann School, a highly respected preparatory institution,

where he polished both his athletic and academic performances. Afterwards he matriculated at Columbia College in 1940. Before leaving Horace Mann, however, his outstanding performances in two key football games had turned what had been viewed as an unprepossessing team into the "heroes of New York City prep football."[9]

He also began to publish fiction in the Horace Mann school magazine. Two samples of these apprentice works—"The Brothers" and "Une Veille de Noel"—have recently been collected. "The Brothers" exploits the familiar "private eye" detective story genre of the 1930s to tell of a successful effort to avert a crime that is not hard for readers to outguess. The other is a slight Greenwich Village Christmas fable that does show an early sympathy with losers. Both are written in a very artificial, formal style that Kerouac would soon abandon.[10]

Jack's actual career at Columbia failed to fulfill the expectations bred by his early feats. Having repressed his literary leanings in order to court fame on the gridiron, he impatiently expected to gain new glory faster than coach Lou Little's game plan allowed. When he was used only sparingly in the first game, Kerouac decided to display some flashy running to attract attention; he ended up breaking his leg in only his third game, so that he spent the rest of the season on the sidelines. In retrospect, one can see that the end of this ill-chosen course was already predictable. Although some almost comic encores followed, it was already clear that Kerouac would never be a successful team player. His subsequent devotion to his literary ambitions in the face of repeated rejections show that he had perseverance, but only when he was calling the plays.

His period of recuperation turned the trick. Since he was still on an athletic scholarship, he was free to return unhampered to his literary pursuits, and during this period he discovered the works of Thomas Wolfe, who was to exercise the most powerful influence on his admirer's first novel. Also just before going back to join the family for the Christmas holidays, Kerouac met Edie Parker, who would subsequently become his first wife. In the spring, he not only continued his own writing, but he also wrote sports columns for the college newspaper. During the summer, he helped the family move from Lowell to New Haven, where his father had found a new job.

Jack reported a day late for football practice in August 1941, but that was only the beginning of his troubles. He was having serious problems communicating with coach Little, and when he saw that he would not get his coveted chance to play in the Columbia-Army game (an old high school foe was on the Army team), he packed up and left the football dormitory, going on the road for the first time on an overnight trip to Washington, D.C., and then returning to join his family in Connecticut. There he got and soon quit a job in a rubber plant. When his father Leo blew up about Jack's ambitions to become a writer, the son obtained a job in a Hartford gas station; but when at Thanksgiving the family decided to move back to Lowell, he rejoined it.

Then on 7 December the Japanese bombed Pearl Harbor, and the United States entered World War II. Kerouac signed up for a navy aviators' program. While waiting to see if he qualified for flying school, he took a job as sports reporter on the *Lowell Sun*. During his three months on this job, he started his first extended work of fiction, using the title *Vanity of Duluoz,* which appeared in print at last as the title of his final major effort. He never completed this book that he modeled on James Joyce's work, because by March he was restless to hit the road again. On a junket to Washington, D.C., however, he found that he was unable to support himself. He was then sworn into the marines while still in the navy program and holding a Coast Guard sailing pass. He served with none of these three branches of the national military, however, but instead took a berth on the *S.S. Dorchester,* a merchant marine cargo vessel headed for Greenland.

Kerouac has written several varying accounts of the *Dorchester* experience, which was generally harrowing for a naive and inexperienced youth. (He once told a shocked British family that he had been "deflowered" by "a nasty, lecherous fatso cook" on that voyage.)[11] He was particularly affected by the sinking of another ship in the convoy with the loss of a thousand men (the *Dorchester* itself was sunk on a subsquent trip). On his return to New York, however, he received eight hundred dollars in back wages, the most money he had ever seen at one time.

Inexplicably, except possibly for the fact that college football teams had been rendered desperate for manpower because of the military draft, he also found waiting for him an invitation from coach Little to rejoin the Columbia team. Once again, however, Kerouac began to feel he was being slighted and, to complicate matters, father Leo appeared to berate Little for not getting him a promised job and not using Jack appropriately. Jack stayed around until the Army game; but the next Monday, while listening to records in his dormitory, he decided to quit the team for good, as he explains in his "Biographical

Resume": "I heard Beethoven [sic] fifth symphony and it had begun to snow and I knew I wanted to be a Beethoven instead of an athlete."[12] He spent the remaining weeks of 1942 sharing an apartment with Edie Parker, who tells of becoming pregnant and being forced to have an abortion, although Kerouac himself nowhere confirms this story.

When in 1943, he at last reported for duty with the navy, he failed the qualifying examination for aviators' training and was sent to a boot camp at Newport, Rhode Island. Although he claims that he scored the highest I.Q. in the history of the base, he found that as a boot he had no status at all and had to obey everyone's orders. Unable to reconcile himself to such rigorous discipline, he dropped his rifle in the middle of a training session and walked off to the library. Although psychiatrists suspected that he had a political motive for feigning insanity, he was given an honorable discharge on psychiatric grounds in June.

For the next year, he divided his time between his parents' new home in Ozone Park, Long Island, and Edie Parker's Manhattan apartment. He took another merchant marine voyage, but was made miserable by a bullying ship's mate. Just when his life seemed to have reached low-water mark, he began to meet the others who would eventually create the Beat Generation.

The first was a Columbia College freshman, Lucien Carr, who believed that he was being pursued with homosexual intent by David Kammerer, a former physical education instructor at Washington University, St. Louis, whom Carr had attracted when he participated in nature walks that Kammerer had led. Kerouac soon formed deeper and more constructive attachments with fellow aspiring writers Allen Ginsberg and William Burroughs, but Carr was to be responsible for one of Kerouac's most traumatic experiences. After Carr, alleging self-defense, stabbed Kammerer to death, Jack was held in a Bronx jail as a material witness. When his family refused to provide bail, he agreed to marry Edie Parker if she would raise the bond from her family. They were married 22 August 1944 and departed for her aunt's home in fashionable Grosse Point, a suburb of Detroit. All charges against Jack were eventually dropped, but Carr was sentenced to a penitentiary term of one to twenty years.

Kerouac stayed in Michigan, working in a factory, long enough to pay off the bond. He then left his new wife there and returned to New York where he shipped out again with the merchant marine; but harassment by another ship's officer caused him to jump ship in Norfolk, Virginia, which ended his merchant marine career. His marriage also broke up, while his ties with Ginsberg and Burroughs strengthened. With the latter he worked on a novel "And the Hippos Were Boiled in Their Tanks," about the Kammerer slaying, but it was never published. Finally Kerouac developed bloodclots in his legs and had to spend most of December 1945 in a veterans' hospital.

Meanwhile his father was dying of cancer. After Leo's death in May 1946 Kerouac settled down to devoting most of that year to writing *The Town and the City*. Ginsberg was back at Columbia, and Burroughs had gone to Texas with his wife. Later in the year, Neal Cassady turned up in New York for the first time and worked as a parking-lot attendant, but on 4 March 1947 he left town again with his wife. In June, Kerouac's only sister, Nin, was married in North Carolina, and when Jack returned to New York, he was promised a merchant marine ship out of San Francisco. He decided to hitchhike to the coast by way of Denver, where Allen Ginsberg was already with Neal Cassady. Thus began the events chronicled in *On the Road*.

On the Road—From Obscurity to Celebrity, 1947–55

The trip began unpropitiously when, after several false starts, a deflated Kerouac had to take a bus to Chicago, where he began hitchhiking to Denver. He met his friends and wound up at last on the West Coast as a security guard in a construction camp; after working there he made his way to Los Angeles and spent two weeks with the young Mexican woman who provided the model for Terry in *On the Road*. Then it was home again by bus to work on his first novel, *The Town and the City,* which he submitted to Scribner's (Thomas Wolfe's publishers) in July 1948, shortly after meeting John Clellon Holmes. By September, Kerouac had revised the first chapter and Macmillan had rejected the novel. Despite the influence of Alfred Kazin, whom Kerouac had met through the New School for Social Research, Scribner's also rejected the novel in December. Undaunted, Kerouac had started to work on the first version of *On the Road* in November.

For Christmas he went with mother Gabrielle to his sister's in North Carolina. Neal Cassady turned up in a new Hudson automobile and the events reflected in the second part of *On the Road* ensued. Kerouac was back in New York in February 1949; in March came word that Harcourt, Brace had accepted *The Town and the City*. Robert Giroux, however, was to make the final decisions on cutting the eleven hundred pages to four hundred, leading Kerouac to observe, "Never again editorship for me."[13] In July, he was off on the third of the journeys that provided the material for *On the Road*. He had also developed enough confidence in the future to discuss taking Edie Parker to Paris in the spring of 1950 and perhaps even providing the money so that Allen Ginsberg could join them.[14]

These plans were shattered after *The Town and the City*, signed John Kerouac, was published on 2 March 1950 and received mixed reviews. The most disheartening experience, however, for Kerouac—like any first novelist—was that after a few weeks sales of the novel simply stopped. His advance had not even been recovered, so that there would be no funds to carry out his grandiose plans. The novel, heavily influenced by Thomas Wolfe, who had enjoyed a considerable revival on college campuses immediately after World War II, was not to the taste of an increasingly neurotic generation, whose romantic impulses were stifled by the increasing paranoia of a witchhunting era. In June, however, Kerouac was off with Neal Cassady on the ill-fated trip to Mexico described in the fourth section of *On the Road*, but he was back by the end of the summer, a disillusioned man.

On 17 November, his earlier marriage to Edie Parker having been annulled, he startled his family and friends by impulsively marrying Joan Haverty, the former girl friend of Bill Cannastra, a proto-Beatnik who had had his head cut off when he stuck it out of a New York City subway car. The following May, Joan announced that she was pregnant, but Kerouac hysterically denied responsibility and continued thereafter to adamantly deny paternity in one of his least attractive displays of childish narcissism. The unacknowledged offspring, Jan Kerouac, has since become a novelist herself.

Kerouac was far more absorbed in the 175,000-word third version of *On the Road*, which he had typed in three weeks beginning 5 April 1951 in a single paragraph on a single scroll of paper. When he delivered it to Robert Giroux's office, Harcourt, Brace rejected it. The strain of incessant typing began to take its toll, and Kerouac was stricken with thrombophlebitis in his legs. He had to spend the summer resting at his sister's home in North Carolina and at a veterans' hospital in the Bronx. In the fall, he moved into an apartment in Richmond Hill on Long Island with his mother.

Of the years that follow, Kerouac wrote in his "Biographical Resume": "spent 6 years on the road writing whatever came into my head, hopping freights, hitchhiking, working as a railroad brakeman, deck hand and scullion on merchant ships, hundreds of assorted jobs, government fire lookout."[15] These peregrinations have been chronicled in bewildering detail by Kerouac's corps of biographers, and there is no point in retracing this path day by weary and often foot-sore day as he swung from New York City to North Carolina to San Jose to Mexico to San Francisco (he even made it at one point to Quebec), often broke, never with a dependable income, trying to place his writings, particularly the versions of *On the Road*. The number of books that he wrote during this period has often been exaggerated, although before September 1955 he had made one of the most important decisions of his life, "to write the Duluoz Legend in sections— instead of as one book,"[16] following the model of Proust. He had also completed *Doctor Sax, Maggie Cassidy, The Subterraneans,* and the "Neal Book," tentatively titled *Visions of Neal* but to emerge finally as *Visions of Cody.* Also during October and November 1951 he had perfected the art of spontaneous "sketching," which he had high hopes would contribute to the spontaneity and immediacy of his Legend. His most complete account of the theory behind this practice is contained in his essay, "Essentials of Spontaneous Prose," which appeared in the *Evergreen Review,* number 5, in 1958.

All through this period Malcolm Cowley tried to provide aid and comfort, but he could not influence Viking Press to take a chance on publishing any of the manuscripts that seemed so daringly unconventional during the dreary Eisenhower years. Through much of this period Kerouac was also engaged, with the aid of Allen Ginsberg and Carl Solomon, in frustrating and finally futile negotiations with Ace Books, publishers of cheap, sensational paperbacks that had accepted William Burrough's *Junkie;* but even Solomon himself (to whom Ginsberg later dedicated *Howl*) showed little more comprehension of what Kerouac was doing than the conservative commercial publishers.

Kerouac did receive an advance of two hundred fifty dollars from Ace early in 1952, probably the largest sum he derived from his writings during the obscure years before 1957, as he was finishing up the "Neal book." He sent this money, however, to his mother and took a mail-handling job with the Southern Pacific Railroad, before entering into a famous ménage à trois with the Cassadys, described in Carolyn's book *Heart Beat* (1976), which in turn became the basis of the poorly received 1978–79 movie with the same title.

When this relationship became too tense, Kerouac went off to Mexico City to visit Burroughs, who the previous year had accidentally shot his wife. Kerouac spent one of his most productive periods there. In five days he wrote a never published novel in French about a meeting in Chinatown with Neal Cassady in 1935 when both were teenagers. He described it as his final resolution of all the plots of *On the Road.*[17] After completing *Doctor Sax,* however, he had a falling out with Burroughs; and, after returning to California, a falling out with the Cassadys that foreshadowed the ruptures that were subsequently to alienate him from all his friends and supporters during his years on the road. He returned East to spend Christmas with his mother.

Early in 1953, before a disillusioning trip to Quebec, he started *Maggie Cassidy* and had an affair with a girl (who has steadily refused to be publicly identified) whom he fictionalized as "Mardou Fox" in *The Subterraneans,* a novel that he reputedly wrote in seventy-two hours in his mother's Richmond Hill apartment. He failed, however, to find a publisher even for this contemporary tale of blighted romance, but before he left New York he embraced the then growing practice of meditation after he read a life of Buddha. Back in California, this proved a new source of friction with the Cassadys, who had also experienced a religious enlightment and had become engrossed with the writings of prophet Edgar Cayce.

Malcolm Cowley told Kerouac that Viking Press might publish *Doctor Sax* if the fantastic sections (which are responsible for its most significant contribution to the Duluoz Legend) were removed, so that it could be offered as a series of sketches of boyhood reminiscences of Lowell; but nothing came of this proposal. Cowley did, however, at last persuade Arabella Porter, dynamic and imaginative editor of New American Library's *New World Writing* (which was during the fifties' doldrums one of the few commercial publications to join the "little magazines" in keeping avant garde writing visible in the United States), to publish in its seventh number "Jazz of the Beat Generation," a passage from *On the Road.* Appearing as the lead article in the issue and signed only "Jean-Louis," this breakthrough piece brought Kerouac one hundred twenty dollars,[18] his first paycheck since 1950, and it gave the first widespread publicity to the term "Beat Generation" (as the novel was then still titled). Two years later Kenneth Rexroth in "Disengagement: The Art of the Beat Generation" (*New World Writing,* no. 11) identified Kerouac as "the most famous 'unpublished' author in America" but appended a footnote that Viking

Press and Grove Press were each planning to publish one of his novels.

Kerouac meanwhile projected a new life of Buddha and was at work selecting materials for his *Book of Dreams.* On 18 January 1955, he had to appear in a New York City court to answer Joan Haverty's suit for nonpayment of child support, but the judge dismissed the case on the grounds of his medical disability. Another trip across the desert brought him back to California, where Allen Ginsberg introduced him to Gary Snyder and where on 13 October 1955 at the Six Gallery, a converted garage on Fillmore Street north of Union in the San Francisco Marina, on a program that also included readings by Philip LaMantia, Michael McClure, Snyder, and Philip Whalen, Allen Ginsberg first publicly performed the recently completed "Howl." Jack Kerouac cheered them on and collected coins from the crowd to buy gallons of California red wine to mellow audience responses. As he later observed in *The Dharma Bums,* the San Francisco Renaissance had begun.

The San Francisco Renaissance, 1955–61

While Kerouac was not an immediate beneficiary of the national attention that began to be focused upon his associates, the reading at the Six marks the turning point in the fortunes of the Beat Generation that turned it into a well publicized, much admired, emulated, and heartily despised institution. After the first reading started "Howl" on its way to immortality, the poem became a national cause célèbre and scandal through a landmark obscenity trial in San Francisco in 1959 that established the importance of expert witnesses in such litigation.[19]

Even Kerouac's own future seemed assured. In July 1955 Malcolm Cowley and editor Keith Jennison had at last prevailed upon Viking Press to accept "The Beat Generation" for publication as *On the Road* two years later, although Cowley insisted upon some revisions, principally cutting down the number of transcontinental trips. In the meantime, an excerpt "The Mexican Girl," appeared in the *Paris Review* in 1955,[20] and Cowley had secured Kerouac an American Academy of Arts and Letters grant of two hundred dollars to work on further projects in Mexico City.

After the celebrated reading, Kerouac remained in Berkeley another six weeks, visiting with Gary Snyder, with whom he made his first mountain-climbing expedition (fictionalized in *The Dharma Bums*). Just as he was preparing to leave, he was shocked by the suicide of Neal Cassady's new girl friend, Natalie Jackson, and he was depressed by a seemingly interminable intercontinental bus ride. Even before *On the Road* appeared, Kerouac was becoming disenchanted with the road life.

Back with his mother again for Christmas in North Carolina, he began work on New Year's Day 1956 on *Visions of Gerard,* a sentimental account of his saintly brother that was to provide the opening section of the Duluoz Legend. In the spring he was back in California, living at Gary Snyder's cabin in Marin County, where he composed at Snyder's behest *The Scripture of the Golden Eternity,* his own version of the Buddhist Diamond Sutra. The work remains one of Kerouac's most obscure, however, because even before it was published by a small press in 1960, Kerouac had abandoned Buddhism. His ambiguous feelings at the time he wrote the work are suggested by the two last of the sixty-six epigrams making up the text. After concluding the description of a long revelation of the Golden Eternity with its first teaching, he writes, "As I regained consciousness I felt so sorry I had a body and a mind suddenly realizing I didnt even have a body and a mind and nothing had ever happened and everything is alright forever and forever and forever," but then he undercuts this transcendental vision with the deflating conclusion that "the second teaching from the golden eternity is that there never was a first teaching from the golden eternity. So be sure."[21]

As Philip Whalen, himself a Buddhist and one of the most perceptive analysts of Kerouac's behavior has observed, his interest in Buddhism was always "pretty much literary."[22] Further evidence of Kerouac's lack of a disposition toward the contemplative life is found in his reaction to the three months of solitude imposed upon him during the summer of 1956 by his job as a fire lookout on Mount Desolation in Washington state—an experience that he fictionalized in *The Dharma Bums* and *Desolation Angels.* He became desperate to find ways to amuse himself until he could escape what was to him awesome confinement.

He fled to Mexico City, where he began *Desolation Angels,* his most journalistic novel, which opened with an account of this experience. He also worked on *Tristessa* until Allen Ginsberg lured him back to New York, where he found that the impending publication of *On the Road* was already making him a media celebrity. In February 1957 he sailed for Tangier to visit William Burroughs. He encountered rough seas and, despite his experience in the merchant marine, he became so upset that his Buddhism vanished under the immediate pressure to be replaced by a "Catholic-like vision of God."[23] In sunny Africa, he suggested the final title for Burroughs's *Naked Lunch,* but suffered his first unhappy experience arising from publishers' treatment of his own work when he found extensive cuts in the text of *The Subterraneans* that was to be printed in the *Evergreen Review.* The project was subsequently scrapped. Before returning to the United States, he spent a few frantic days as a tourist in France, but he never acquired the manner for the international road.

Another dismal and expensive disaster was an attempt to move his mother to California. Gabrielle did not like the foggy Bay area, and they remained only six weeks, just long enough for their furniture to arrive in time to be shipped back. Before they left, however, advance copies of *On the Road* had arrived at a time when Neal Cassady was visiting. A coolness developed between the originals of Dean and Sal in the novel, and Kerouac never got his relationship with Cassady back on the old basis.

On 5 September 1957, *On the Road* was published, but this long-anticipated event failed to change the deteriorating course of the author's life. He was even less prepared for success and celebrity than he had been for failure and obscurity. The furor surrounding the book caught him completely by surprise, and he was as dismayed by the discourtesy of admirers who invaded his home and stole his belongings as he was by the reviewers who attacked him mercilessly as the apostle of a dissolute life-style. He apparently never realized that any sensationally popular new work is going to be bitterly controversial, and he expressed his dismay in the "Biographical Resume" that he sent at the time to Donald Allen: "I have been writing my heart out all my life, but only getting a living out of it now, and the attacks are coming in thick. A lot of people are mad and jealous and bitter and I only hope they also can be heard by an expanding publishing program the size of Russia's."

"I am only a jolly storyteller," he concluded, "and have nothing to do with politics or schemes and my only plan is the old Chinese Way of the Tao: 'avoid the authorities' ";[24] but that is not the way he was seen by the angry antagonists representing what smirking *Life* magazine called "Beatsville" and "Squaresville." Kerouac's novel proved the spark that ignited the battle that had long been brewing underground between angry youths who felt oppressed and senile bigots.

Kerouac was already beginning, however, to lean enough toward "Squaresville" himself to write on 24 August to Peter Orlovsky that he and Burroughs were really Faustian personalities who had reached the end of their ropes.[25] He spoke ruefully of being "universally attacked" at an ill-advised week of readings at the trendy Village Vanguard in New York, where his supporters could not afford the prices. Public appearances always distressed him, and he responded by increasing his drinking—his method from this time forward of coping with unmanageable problems. He was inspired to dash off a three-act play, *The Beat Generation,* which has not been produced. Its last act provided, however, the basis for Robert Frank's short film, *Pull My Daisy,* for which Kerouac wrote and delivered the overvoiced narration. Negotiations to sell the movie rights to *On the Road,* however, fell through, though, ironically; as Tom Clark points out, after Kerouac's death his estate made a deal with Francis Ford Coppola for the rights that brought in more money than Kerouac had made in his lifetime.[26] (The film has yet to be made.) Finally Kerouac canceled all promotional events and fled home to his mother in Florida to begin work on an evocation of his childhood just after brother Gerard's death. To be called "Memory Babe," this work was never completed. When Malcolm Cowley asked Kerouac for a book that would prove another best-seller, he dashed off *The Dharma Bums,* composing it as he had *On the Road* on one long paper scroll and completing it in ten marathon typing sessions. Ultimately he was displeased with the result and vowed to write no more potboilers on others' commissions. In fact, he completed no major works for another four years.

The demoralizing effects of celebrity mounted. When *The Subterraneans* appeared in 1958, it was cut to pieces by the reviewers, but the movie rights brought fifteen thousand dollars, the largest single sum he had yet been paid. In April 1958 he was beaten up outside his favorite Kettle of Fish bar on McDougall Street in Greenwich Village, while his new home on Long Island was overrun by curiosity seekers. The celebrity served Neal Cassady even worse; he was arrested by the California police and sentenced to five years in San Quentin prison for possessing marijuana.

The Dharma Bums received cruel and contemptuous treatment when it was published in October, and other writers turned on this new threat to their eminence. Truman Capote made his famous crack that Kerouac's books were not writing, but typing, and John Updike mercilessly—but with considerable justification—satirized *On the Road* as juvenile in the *New Yorker* ("On the Sidewalk," 21 February 1959). Kerouac was infuriated by references to his dependence on his mother, who was indeed trying to break up his relationships with his Beat friends.

Jack's behavior deteriorated, and he worried and alienated many of his friends by his increasingly heavy drinking. Robert Frank barred him from the set where *Pull My Daisy* was being filmed, for example; but at least the backlog of novels composed during his years of penury were getting into print, even if reviewers were not receiving them enthusiastically. *Doctor Sax* and *Mexico City Blues,* a collection of poems, appeared in 1959, along with a selection of passages from *Visions of Cody* in a now much sought after limited edition. (New Directions was unwilling to take a chance on the complete long, unconventional text, and it was not published until after Kerouac's death.) None impressed reviewers, however, and when *Maggie Cassidy* appeared as an inexpensive paperback, it was either ignored or attacked. In April 1959 Kerouac also started writing a series of columns for *Escapade,* one of the gingerly risqué magazines that emerged in the wake of the success of Hugh Hefner's *Playboy,* that have never been collected.

Yet one glorious episode, which Beats' historians have generally ignored, made 1959 a happy time in which the antiestablishment Beats came as close as their distrust of organizations permitted to functioning as a group. Most of the leading figures associated with the Beat Generation—Kerouac, Allen Ginsberg, Philip Whalen, Philip LaMantia, John Kelly—were all in San Francisco. One day in May at Cassandra's Coffee House, they came up with the idea of printing *Beatitude,* a mimeographed "weekly miscellany of poetry and other jazz designed to extol beauty and promote the beatific life among the various mendicants, neo-existentialists, christs, poets, painters, musicians and other inhabitants and observers of North Beach"[27] under the editorship of Bob Kaufman.

The venture survived for sixteen issues, including a delightful Fourth of July parody number. With the eighth issue, *Beatitude* (the name was pronounced Beat'-i-tude) moved to Pierre Delattre's Bread and Wine Mission, a principal Beat rendezvous in North Beach, but by issue 16, "the Mission was dead and most of the early contributors had made off to faraway scenes."[28] A continuation was promised under the editorship of Jory Sherman, but it soon petered out. The Beat movement had climaxed; *Beatitude* was its rare, brief, and shamefully ignored flowering. The moment that created it could not be sustained longer than a single San Francisco summer. By 1960, the Beats had indeed dispersed; the action was over in North Beach, though Lawrence Ferlinghetti's City Lights Bookshop and Vesuvio's bar across the alley continue to mark the spot as the liveliest kind of monuments.

After leaving San Francisco near the end of 1959, Jack Kerouac returned to his mother's home, at that moment in Northport, Long Island. They had been scuttling aimlessly between Florida and New York, since he had begun to earn some money, without being able to settle upon a mutually agreeable location.

Tristessa appeared in a cheap paperback in 1960 and was simply ignored by reviewers. The movie version of *The Subterraneans,* starring George Peppard and Leslie Caron, was so much changed from the novel that it embarrassed Kerouac's Beat friends without pleasing many filmgoers. Kerouac was becoming so depressed that he tried to get away from all his problems by taking a solitary vacation at Ferlinghetti's cabin in Bixby Canyon in the Big Sur country. Here occurred the nervous breakdown that is chronicled in *Big Sur,* the novel that is the chronological conclusion of the Duluoz Legend. Once again Kerouac found that he could not endure solitude, so he fled back to the city and began drinking heavily. He became involved also in a sordid affair with Neal Cassady's latest mistress. Her visit to Ferlinghetti's cabin with her four-year-old son precipitated the dreadful weekend that ended altogether Kerouac's attachment to Buddhism (and to Beat associations generally) and drove him back to the Roman Catholic faith of his childhood with a vision like the one that ends *The Subterraneans.*

His intellectual and spiritual breakdowns were accompanied by physical deterioration as well. Michael McClure observes that at Big Sur, Jack had already lost some of his "personal grace through booze." He had become "physically less attractive."[29]

Back in New York in January 1961 Kerouac participated with Allen Ginsberg in Timothy Leary's psychedelic experiments, but this attempt to curb Kerouac's alcoholism was a disaster that years later he described as his undoing. In July he went back to Mexico City to complete the second part of *Desolation Angels,* his first major piece of writing since 1957. Back in Florida his increasingly serious drinking led to a minor abdominal hemorrhage, but he managed to taper off enough by October to write *Big Sur,* the account of his breakdown the year before, in ten days on a continuous teletype roll. Then he headed north to look for a property to buy in Vermont, but he soon ended up in New York City on a thirty-day drinking bout, during which he met Joan Haverty for the first time in six years and was introduced to the nine-year-old daughter whose parentage he steadfastly denied. At the long avoided court hearing, he was ordered to pay fifty-two dollars a week child support until Jan was twenty-one.

This defeat marked the low point of Kerouac's psychic battle for transcendence. The Beat movement, which he had disowned anyway, was dead insofar as it had ever been a movement. Largely media-made, the Beat Generation, like many regenerative attempts to combat America's increasing materialism, had been embalmed by 1960 as an academic property by documentary collections like Gene Feldman and Max Gartenberg's *The Beat Generation and the Angry Young Men* (1958), Seymour Krim's *The Beats* (1960), and especially Thomas Parkinson's *A Casebook on the Beat* (1961), which snippetized the movement for convenient anthologizing.

Premature Retirement and Death in the Sunshine State, 1961–69 (and beyond)

For a while Kerouac's energies seemed to be regenerating as he settled down in Florida to retype *Big Sur* in conventional form and send it, along with *Visions of Gerard,* to Farrar, Straus, where his old supporter Robert Giroux had moved, but Kerouac was soon back on the bottle and Gabrielle grew restless once more. In November, Jack bought a modern house in Northport, Long Island. In the meantime *Big Sur* had been published, but attracted little response from reviewers and readers who failed to grasp the significance of this account of an artist's crack-up.

Understandably depressed, Kerouac planned a dark history of the downfall of his family and turned repentantly to the trappings of his childhood Roman Catholic faith. A visit with Neal Cassady failed to reinvigorate their friendship, and a serious effort to stop drinking was thwarted by the cold and uncomprehending review of the work perhaps closest to Kerouac's heart, *Visions of Gerard.*[30]

In 1964 Cassady turned up again as the bus driver for the transcontinental trip of Ken Kesey and the Merry Pranksters. Cassady lured Kerouac to a party to celebrate the publication of Kesey's second novel, *Sometimes a Great Notion.* Tom Wolfe reports that "Kesey and Kerouac didn't say much to each other. . . . Here was Cassady in between them, once the mercury for Kerouac and the whole Beat Generation and now the mercury for Kesey and the whole—what?— something wilder and weirder out on the road. It was like hail and farewell. Kerouac was the old star. Kesey was the wild new comet from the West heading christ knew where."[31]

The occasion provides a key to understanding Kerouac's last (to use his own favorite word) sad days. Whether Kerouac could recognize it or not, in *One Flew over the Cuckoo's Nest,* Kesey had written the heroic account of the triumph of the individual over the system that readers thought they had found in *On the Road.* But Kerouac's work was elegiac and defeatist; whereas Kesey's was defiant and hopeful. Kesey was mistakenly taken for Kerouac's disciple to the vast annoyance of both; no wonder Kerouac displayed hostility when he contemplated Kesey enjoying so quickly the success that he had waited for so long and then so little enjoyed, as well as Kesey's promoting a kind of anarchic activism that disturbed Kerouac's basically passive personality.

The vision of *Cuckoo's Nest* is that transcendence of the spirit-destroying inertia of the "combine" demanded self-sacrifice (on the part of McMurphy) to trigger another's liberation (Chief Bromden's); but Kerouac could face neither martyrdom (though he ultimately imposed an inglorious one upon himself) nor the liberation that meant breaking with Gabrielle, the pale ghost of Gerard, and the whole weight of the accusing past.

At this point disaster struck at home to strengthen even further Gabrielle's determined hold on her remaining child (who in her eyes had been set upon by devils). After Kerouac's brother-in-law requested a divorce, sister Caroline suffered a fatal heart attack.[32]

A small compensation was that the diminished family had some money again. Although *Desolation Angels* was poorly received at the height of the era of the Hippie flower children, Bantam Books purchased the paperback rights for fifty thousand dollars, Kerouac's first substantial earnings in several years. He also received a seventy-five-hundred-dollar advance for *Vanity of Duluoz* and was able to project a six-month trip to France to study his family's origins. The trip proved, however, a ten-day disaster. Kerouac behaved like the stereotype of the ugly American tourist, stayed drunk most of the time, and then retreated to the United States to give his version of what happened in the disappointingly obscure *Satori in Paris.*

During 1966 he was on the house-hunting road again. Gabrielle wanted to go back to New England, and he purchased a home in Hyannis, Massachusetts, by then famous as the Kennedy family summer compound. Here Mémère, as Kerouac affectionately called his mother, suffered a stroke that immobilized her for the rest of her life and kept Jack even closer to home than he had been during the past decade. To pay her medical expenses, he arranged a lecture tour of Italy, which he endured only by drinking his way through it. On his return he married Stella Sampas, the older sister of one of his greatest friends from Lowell, Sebastian (Sammy) Sampas.[33] She was to prove both caretaker and bodyguard for Jack and his mother during their last painful years.

Even the watchful Stella, however, could not prevent Jack from being arrested several times for public drunkenness on image-conscious Cape Cod. Kerouac tried to avoid further embarrassments by going home at first to Lowell, where he bought a house in the most expensive section of town. He was avoided by his old French-Canadian cronies, but was welcomed into and protected by Stella's large family of Greek descent.

The move did inspire a last burst of writing. In March 1967 he returned to the title conceived long ago, *Vanity of Duluoz,* for the long-planned tragic family history that was essentially a retracing of the ground covered by his first published novel, *The Town and the City.* He completed the novel by May in ten furious bursts of writing between long rests. Published the next year by Coward-McCann, it attracted more favorable attention than his other recent publications, but proved a commercial failure.

By this time Kerouac had broken with all his former Beat sidekicks, denouncing Allen Ginsberg on William Buckley's "Firing Line" program in the fall of 1968. Then on 3 February 1968 Neal Cassady died of congestive heart failure after overindulging at a wedding party in San Miguel de Allende, Mexico. Despite the cooling of their relationship and a subsequent long separation, Kerouac could not accept Neal/Dean/Cody's having reached the end of the road.

He rallied enough, however, to enjoy at last a short trip abroad to Spain, Portugal, and Germany with old friends from Lowell and to make yet another move, at Gabrielle's prodding, back to Florida. They settled in St. Petersburg in November 1968, but they had run out of money, and Stella had to take a factory job. Kerouac fished from the careful files that he had always maintained of his writings one of the early 1950 versions of *On the Road* about a teenaged Negro named Pictorial Review Jackson. Adding a new ending, he submitted it for publication as *Pic.*

He was never to see it in print. To raise some money quickly, he accepted a commission from the ultraconservative *Chicago Tribune* to write a piece that was subsequently syndicated nationally, "After Me, the Deluge." This was a misogynistic diatribe against Allen Ginsberg, Ken Kesey, Timothy Leary, and the other members of a now flourishing counterculture with which he refused to be identified. His outward appearance began to reflect his internal disintegration, and he took some harsh beatings after provoking hostile confrontations in sleazy Tampa bars. "I think I'll drop out," was his final message to the world. He did not realize how far out or how soon.

On 20 October 1969 cirrhosis of the liver caused fatal hemorrhaging. Few came to the Florida wake, but Ginsberg, Peter Orlovsky, and Gregory Corso turned up at the second one in Lowell, where Kerouac was buried in the Sampas family plot.

His presiding spirit lives on in the Jack Kerouac School of Disembodied Poetics at the Naropa Institute, Boulder, Colorado, where the long list of teacher-gurus includes Amiri Baraka, William Burroughs, Gregory Corso, Robert Duncan, Allen Ginsberg, Ken Kesey, Michael McClure, and even "Jack Kerouac, Disembodied."[34] He has also been, among other things, the subject of a ten-day conference at the University of Colorado-Boulder, 23 July–1 August 1982, celebrating the twenty-fifth anniversary of the publication of *On the Road.* All the surviving celebrities of the Beat Generation were there; they had remained true to Kerouac's memory even after he had disavowed them.

Chapter Two
Breaking the Print Barrier
The Town and the City (1950)

If the literary reputation of John Kerouac, as he signed his first published novel in 1950, depended upon *The Town and the City,* his name would certainly be as lost to history as those of many other aspiring writers who break into print every year, to be indifferently received and never heard from again. The artistic merits of the novel are adequately suggested by a brief, anonymous notice in the *New Yorker:* "Mr. Kerouac's . . . habit of using ten words where one would do inclines the reader to put the book aside until some day when there is absolutely nothing else around to read."[1] There is no need to elaborate; such interest as the book possesses is the result of the very different body of work that its author subsequently signed Jack Kerouac.

Since the novel is of little intrinsic merit, it warrants scrutiny decades later only for the light it may shed upon the author and his later well-publicized writings. The novel cannot be considered as part of the Duluoz Legend because of the drastic differences between the Martin family in the novel and Kerouac's own and of the addition to this family chronicle of many purely invented incidents, unparalleled by any in the Kerouacs' history. *The Town and the City* remains uniquely valuable, however, because of the changes in the treatment of autobiographical material in this isolated apprentice work and in subsequent contributions to the Legend, especially Kerouac's last major novel, *Vanity of Duluoz,* which covers roughly the same period from the mid-1930s to the mid-1940s.

The powerful influence of Thomas Wolfe upon the early novel is immediately apparent. Although Kerouac had not discovered Wolfe until he was eighteen in 1940 at Columbia College, he had quickly become a devotee of the North Carolinian's epic prose poems, so that when he began transforming his own experiences into fiction he turned to Wolfe as a model.

As the *New Yorker* review suggests, however, Kerouac had not really learned the principal lesson that Wolfe's works had to teach. Fascinated by the bulk, the dynamism, and the superficially bombastic style of Wolfe's productions, Kerouac failed to appreciate the nature of the impetus that drove Wolfe on the same kind of self-destructive quest that Kerouac himself was launching. He imitated Wolfe's rhapsodic manner and hypnotized fascination with the mysteriousness of life; but Kerouac's book lacked any center, for he had not realized the importance of Wolfe's concept of himself as attributed to his alter ego Eugene Gant in *Look Homeward, Angel:* "It was not his quality as a romantic to escape out of life, but into it . . . his fantasies found extension in reality."[2] Kerouac was not engaged in the kind of quest for "an unfound door" that motivated Wolfe, who like Fitzgerald's Jay Gatsby could never really accept his family. Kerouac—and his fictional alter egos—instead constantly return to the family, even though readers may find his disreputable friends and exotic lovers like Mardou Fox more interesting.

One of the major problems with *The Town and the City,* in fact, is that the Martin family, which Kerouac in *Book of Dreams* calls "the Kerouacs of my soul,"[3] appears to be based not on his own small family, but on Wolfe's much larger fictional Gant family, modeled on *his* own. Kerouac expanded his one brother who died in childhood and one sister into a family of nine. Curiously none of the three sisters in the Martin family corresponds in either her position in the family or her personality to Kerouac's only sister Caroline (Nin); but a most important linkage between the Gant and Martin families in the novels is that in both there is a set of male twins, one of which, the most beloved of all the family, dies in childhood. Kerouac's most drastic departure from Wolfe's model, however, was one that would have scandalized the North Carolinian. Rather than basing a single central figure that dominates the novel upon himself as Wolfe had Eugene Gant, Kerouac split himself into two brothers—Peter, the fourth eldest of six brothers and the one who shares Kerouac's athletic career, and Francis, an intellectual who is the surviving member of the slightly older pair of twins. Through this device, Kerouac was able to turn a character who shared many of his own experiences into a literal twin of the character based on his own brother Gerard, with whom Ti Jean Duluoz, Jack's alter ego in *Visions of Gerard,* for the first four years of his life identified himself.

Kerouac himself acknowledged in a letter to an admirer in November 1950 that he was both Peter and Francis in the novel and even went on to suggest that he was also the oldest brother Joe,[4] though in the course of the novel, the reader finds that Joe increasingly takes on the characteristics of Neal Cassady. While Kerouac admitted that he had divided specific experiences of his own between the characters, he provided no clue to the reasons for the division. Even if he were entirely conscious of these reasons, to confess them would probably have been to give away too much about his self-image.

The artistic consequences of this personality splitting were disastrous, for neither Peter nor Francis emerges as a complex enough individual to be believable (it is difficult even to determine the exact difference in their ages, although Francis appears to have been a year ahead of Peter in school). Rather they seem to be doppelgängers, each complete only when matched with his complement. This dubious narrative device proves, however, of inestimable value in gaining insight into Kerouac's often tortured and contradictory personality.

Most of Kerouac's own actions and achievements are attributed to Peter, who is, as Jack was, thirteen years old at the time the action begins in 1935. This thoroughly nice boy and devoted son is a gifted football player who becomes a local hero when he scores the winning touchdown in the high school's big Thanksgiving Day game with its traditional rival. He is the one who moves on to the Ivy League on an athletic scholarship (though to the University of Pennsylvania rather than Columbia) and finally quits the team (though Beethoven plays no part in this decision; Peter returns home to help support the family). He joins the merchant marine during World War II and becomes a crony of the Beat crowd to whom he is introduced by Levinsky-Ginsberg. It is his friend Alex who dies in the Italian campaign during the war, and he who remains at home during his father's dying days. All these were things that Kerouac felt he could admit with pride, if some sorrow.

Kerouac, however, attributes to Francis two of his most traumatic emotional experiences about which he later felt embarrassed or uncomfortable—the high school love affair that later provides the basis for *Maggie Cassidy* and the devastating experience at navy boot camp that led to his refusal to accept military discipline and ultimately his psychiatric discharge from the service.

By assigning these two unpleasant episodes to the restless intellectual Francis, Kerouac is able to allow Peter to remain a "regular fellow," a kind of Tom Sawyer to his brother's Huck Finn. Most of Francis's other important experiences, however—his friendship with a mysterious Wilfred Engels, whom he meets in a bookstore, his attending and graduating from Harvard, and his working in a music store to support himself while in Cambridge have no counterparts in Kerouac's career. Are these what he would have liked to imagine himself doing?

Francis's attending Harvard poses a particular problem to the credibility of the novel, as he is supposedly supported by his father, who is also represented as constantly financially distressed, as Leo Kerouac actually was. Later Francis lives in Greenwich Village, not Morningside Heights, with a glamorous mistress and is last seen departing after World War II to study in Paris at the Sorbonne. While Peter at the end of the novel chooses to come home to his dying father and assume the paternal role after the father's death, Francis, who has earlier announced that he does not belong at home, in one of the most emotionally charged scenes in the novel, snubs the father and breaks with the family to go abroad, one gathers, permanently.

Was Kerouac himself torn by a desire to make a similar break? Was one part of him in a Joycean revolt against family, country, and church (or any other institutions), while another was from childhood conservative, traditional, and devoted to a rural patriarchal life? While Kerouac must have quite deliberately divided his own experiences between his characters, it is not clear from the novel or his comments the extent to which he understood the basis for his choices. Peter, as he explains in one of his rare conversations with Francis, has "a lot of ideas," but "never can put them together nice and logical."[5] These few conversations, although probably only by hindsight, leave the reader with the eerie impression of someone talking to himself, one part arguing with the other about the difficulty of making a choice between options that create inner conflicts.

The basic split between them is brought out in their longest confrontation when both return home from college—Francis from his second year at Harvard, Peter from his freshman year at Penn. The cynical Francis attacks his confused brother:

Isn't it true that all they told you when you were a kid turned out to be a lot of crap? They told you about God as soon as you had Santa Claus in doubt or before, *someone* did. Yet you ought to know by now there's no Godliness anyway, and there certainly is no God to comfort and watch over us. . . . Surely at some time it'll occur to you that love's just a word describing the fiddling around with flattery and deceit that makes you feel a little better for a moment. And then justice. . . . Men are too unhappy for *that*! (157)

Peter refuses to believe what Francis says, but Kerouac comments in conclusion that this was "a strange conversation that Peter never forgot."

Since Kerouac either invented or transcribed from some internal dialogue this pronouncement, he could obviously take the position of a tough, cynical sophisticate who longed to make a complete break with his environment and yet identify himself with another figure who could not accept such thoughts. A constantly raging conflict between the twins imprisoned in one body could well account for Kerouac's restless wanderings, punctuated by retreats to his home and mother, his seemingly inexplicable rages, and his withdrawal at last from a world that he had helped to form and then found distasteful. "Peter" and "Francis" must have warred constantly for domination over Kerouac's thoughts and actions, and this struggle was to play a major role in the shaping of the Duluoz Legend.

It is difficult to pull together the disparate parts of the Legend because of the irreconcilability of the attitudes expressed by the controlling narrative voices. In *The Town and the City*, by dividing the portrayal of himself between the two brothers, Kerouac was able to give the third-person narrator a distance from the action that made possible an equilibrium in the treatment of the conflicting parts of his own personality; but in the later works, which are dominated by a single autobiographically based figure, often a first-person narrator, control of the attitudes shaping the narrative depended upon which of the conflicting elements within the author was momentarily in control. (Perhaps the marathon typing sessions that resulted in the published version of *On the Road, The Subterraneans, The Dharma Bums,* and *Big Sur,* for example, were in part attributable to the determination of the "voice" in control to get its piece said while it remained dominant.)

It is important in understanding the spectrum of Kerouac's temperament from Beat rebellion to traditional French-Canadian conservatism to bear in mind that "Peter" generally prevailed, although Francis asserted himself during those bleak periods in the 1950s (especially in *Doctor Sax, Maggie Cassidy, Tristessa*) when Kerouac tried to write himself out of obscurity. Ultimately Peter won the battle—as the relative importance assigned to the two roles in the first prophetic novel foreshadowed—but at a terrible price. "Francis" was vanquished at last, but his haunting voice remained powerful enough to drive Peter, quite literally, to drink. One can only muse about what would have happened had Francis prevailed and launched Kerouac on a career that would have paralleled James Joyce's or Henry Miller's search for intellectual fulfillment in expatriation.

In any event, *The Town and the City* is of unique importance in evaluating Kerouac's attempted legendizing of his own life because of its revelation of the author's apparently only partly conscious projection of a split personality that would never find a total resolution. In order to make the Legend fully succeed, the writer would have had to remain thoroughly conscious of this internal division and make its consequences one of the principal themes of his chronicle.

While the wordiness of most of the novel as published leaves little doubt of the publisher's wisdom in cutting the original eleven hundred pages to four hundred, it would be useful indeed to have the complete original text available to contemplate the question of the relative roles of Peter and Francis. Was what was eliminated (reputedly more than half the manuscript) devoted to further characterization of them or to further adventures of the other characters, especially the numerous siblings who are of relatively little interest? (Much space even in the published version is devoted to the youngest brother, Mickey, who is strongly reminiscent of the sentimental characters in William Saroyan's *The Human Comedy*.)[6] It is doubtful, however, that the basic pattern of Peter's movement back toward his family roots and Francis's away from them would be found much altered.

A final curious feature of this episodic family chronicle is that the single most effective piece of writing in it is a two-page vignette of two cynical bulldozer operators' discovery of brother Charley Martin's dead body on a battlefield in Okinawa. This sketch concerns a character who had no counterpart in reality (he is the brother between Peter and Mickey, who is never consistently developed, possibly as a result of the extensive cuts), and it is set in a locale that Kerouac had never seen, involving a life-style that he could only imagine; yet it is one of his most memorable short sketches. Again one can only vainly speculate what he might have achieved had he been able to reconcile the split between the gentle, nostalgic Peter and the tough, ambitious Francis, overcoming his overpoweringly narcissistic obsession with himself and giving full vent to his imaginative powers to reconstruct with the sardonic power he displays here situations beyond the limits of his own experience.

The title of this early novel, however, reflects the same dichotomy

as that posed by the two principal characters. Francis represents the
"city," not even ultimately Cambridge or New York, but legendary
Paris, while Peter embodies the town, observing that "the best kind
of life, as far as I'm concerned, was the life we used to live on my
grandfather's farm in New Hampshire" (411). He embraces this view
when he sees "as in an ancient vision spaded up from his being, what
life must be about, at last. He saw that it was love and work and true
hope" (472). Kerouac himself finally made the same decision when he
rejected his Beat associates for life with mother, though by the time
he did, it was too late to accomplish much work or to justify much
hope.

John Clellon Holmes's *Go* (1952)

Kerouac has the unusual distinction of having attracted more attention at the beginning of his career as the basis for a fictional character
in a friend's novel than through his own work. In what is generally
regarded as the most authentic portrayal of the origins of the Beat
Generation in New York City, John Clellan Holmes's *Go,* published
in 1952, Kerouac provides the model for Gene Pasternak.

Kerouac collaborated with Holmes when both were working on
their first novels, but later he came to resent Holmes's more immediate success. Certainly the picture of him in what has proved Holmes's
only memorable novel does not correspond with that of either of the
Martin brothers in *The Town and the City* or the idealized portrait of
Ti Jean that emerges from the various components of the Duluoz Legend. Gene Pasternak is, in fact, not even as important a character in
Go as David Levinsky, based on Allen Ginsberg, whom Holmes knew
better and actually found more interesting because of his Blakean visions that are discussed at length in *Go.* The main story line of the
novel concerns the marital adjustment problems of Paul and Kathryn
Hobbes, based on Holmes and his wife; the emerging Beat commu-
nity provides only a backdrop for this uptight couple's descent
through a modern hell.

As Pasternak, Kerouac emerges as a figure somewhat resembling
Peter Martin in *The Town and the City,* who embraces at the end of
the novel the kind of pastoral vision that Peter had in Kerouac's
novel. "I want to get married," he tells Hobbes soon after their meeting, "get settled, maybe have a big farm and kids and everything."[7]

He expresses also in this novel set in the late 1940s the same surprising conservatism that Kerouac exhibited in his later years, when he explains, for example, that he doesn't like "all that free-love stuff, that liberal bohemianism, between friends. It isn't right, or straight" (204).

Pasternak's actions belie these words, however; he is pictured principally as an aggressive, inconsiderate womanizer, who, despite his protestations against free love, initiates an affair with a mixed-up young married woman, Christine, who is bored and unhappy because her mechanic husband neglects her. Before pursuing this affair, Pasternak brings another young woman to the Hobbes's apartment, but is frustrated when she declares that she is a virgin who feels nothing when she gives him some unspecified form of "satisfaction." He becomes very deeply involved, however, with Christine, who wants to have an affair and run off with him to San Francisco. When she becomes pregnant, though, he denies that he is responsible (just as Kerouac himself did when his wife Joan Haverty became pregnant) and breaks off his relationship with her. As Kathryn Hobbes had predicted, Pasternak's callous behavior drives Christine to tell her husband about the affair with Pasternak, omitting the fact that they actually committed adultery. When last heard from, Christine has dropped the whole "Beat" circle and is being counseled by a "quack psychiatrist" in the Bronx's Grand Concourse. When Pasternak inscribes on the Hobbes's bathroom wall, "Gene cons Christine," Kathryn grabs the pencil, crosses out "Christine" and substitutes "everybody" (184), yet only a little later she goes to bed with Pasternak herself, though she admits to her husband that it was a silly thing to do.

Holmes admits in an introduction to a reprint of the novel in 1976 that "the only completely invented incident in the book is when Pasternak sleeps with Kathryn," but he adds that he put it in because it seemed "thematically correct."[8] Evidently he feels that it set the stage for a melodramatic reconciliation between the couple from whose lives Pasternak soon thereafter disappears, following the fantastic coincidence (that is based on an actual happening) of Pasternak's first novel being accepted for publication on the same day that Hobbes's is turned down. (Despite Kerouac's initial advantage through this turn of events, he became jealous and resentful when Holmes's novel was published later, received better reviews, and for a while sold better.

He probably also resented Holmes's unflattering portrayal of his treatment of women—one that seems to have been, like many of Holmes's observations, accurate.)

Holmes's novel is valuable not only for this characterization of Kerouac, which has to be taken into consideration when evaluating Kerouac's self-portrait in his own novels, but also for its presentation of the ambience of the embryonic Beat Generation. Holmes claims in his introduction to the reprint that "even whole conversations are verbatim," and the artistic weakness of his work is that vast stretches of it seem just stenography. It is also the first work to introduce the term "Beat Generation," though Holmes carefully attributes it to Pasternak/Kerouac. About halfway through the novel, speaking skeptically of a character based on Neal Cassady, Kathryn Hobbes observes that he does not want to lose his wife's salary: "Oh, he cares about those things, no matter what he *says!* It's been two weeks and I'll bet he hasn't even been looking [for work]. That's the *beat* generation for you" (166, Holmes's italics).

To Gene Pasternak is attributed a more comprehensive view of the rising phenomenon: "You know, everyone I know is kind of furtive, kind of beat. They all go along the street like they were guilty of something, but didn't believe in guilt. I can spot them immediately! And it's happening all over the country, to everyone; a sort of revolution of the soul, I guess *you'd* call it!" (36).

Hobbes/Holmes's own benediction at the end of *Go* on the people he has met and the events he has become involved in is less equivocally upbeat. He observes of the graffiti on the slimy walls of a run-down bar in Hoboken: "There loneliness scribbled a lewd invitation; desire chalked out a vulgar sketch; frustrate tenderness turned cruel with mockery; ungiven love became a feverish obscenity. All, all . . . blunt confessions of longing, words as would be written on the walls of hell. He was paralyzed with a vision of unending lovelessness" (310, Holmes's ellipsis).

Chapter Three
On the Road
Work in Progress

At the beginning of *Big Sur* (1962), Jack Kerouac departs from his usual practice to add a prefatory note in which he explains that *"My work comprises one vast book like Proust's except that my remembrances are written on the run instead of afterwards in a sick bed. . . . In my old age I intend to collect all my work and re-insert my pantheon of uniform names, leave the long shelf full of books there, and die happy."*

This "enormous comedy" he called the Duluoz Legend. He never lived into old age, when the proposed collection would have been made with *Big Sur* as the last major section; nor does he appear to have died happy. We would surely have a different concept of Kerouac's intentions and achievement if his lifelong "work in progress" had received this final editing; as things stand, we must fit the pieces together for ourselves.

Certainly some of his novels would not be included, at least in their present forms. His last major completed work, *Vanity of Duluoz,* superseded his first published novel, *The Town and the City,* which could never have been made compatible with the later works because of the major differences between the wholly invented Martin family and the mirror image of his own family found in the later novels.

The Subterraneans and *The Dharma Bums* were prompted by quite different motivations from the other novels and would require rewriting beyond a simple substitution of a uniform set of names. The posthumous *Pic,* as it stands, has no relationship at all to the other works. Kerouac's most popular and celebrated novel, *On the Road,* was also in his eyes superseded long before it was published, as it was only one of the stages of a work in progress that he considered to have achieved its final form in *Visions of Cody,* which was never published in its entirety during his lifetime. What was at last published as *On the Road* had been completed in 1951 and had circulated for years under the title "The Beat Generation." Tim Hunt in the most brilliant scholarly study so far of any of Kerouac's works, *Kerouac's Crooked Road* (1981), presents a convincing theory about the relationships between the various—and often greatly different—versions of what Kerouac conceived as a work in progress that found its final form only in *Visions of Cody* (earlier referred to as the "Neal Book").

The preliminary version, however, that Kerouac reputedly typed in a single paragraph on a single scroll of paper in April 1951 is the one that has become a modern classic, overshadowing all of what the author considered the more definitive chronicles of the Legend of Ti Jean Duluoz. The principal questions that must be faced are: why has this become and remained so much more popular than any other of Kerouac's works, and what does its popularity suggest about the sensibilities of its audience?

An Episodic Tale

One of the features that conspicuously differentiates *On the Road* from Kerouac's other works is its structure. After establishing a reputation with this work, Kerouac was increasingly able to insist upon his books being published just as he had written them. Astute editor Malcolm Cowley, however, who was instrumental in Viking Press's finally publishing *On the Road,* forced Kerouac to accept some changes in the work. While the unavailability of the manuscripts makes it impossible even to guess how much these changes may have affected the contents and tone of the work, we know from Allen Ginsberg's comments, for example, that in the episode in part three in a Sacramento motel,[1] Cowley insisted on the deletion of mention of Dean Moriarity's permitting the owner of an automobile to fellate him in order to take control of the car for the rest of the trip.

Cowley told Ann Charters, however, that all the changes he suggested "were big ones, mostly omissions. I said why don't you boil down these to two or three trips and keep the mood of the content." The aim of the changes, he said, was to "make it a more continuous narrative. . . . Kerouac agreed and did the job."[2]

Tom Clark minimizes the possible importance of these changes by commenting that, although Kerouac complained that "the published version was an emasculation of the 1951 book . . . Viking's 1956 editing left the story intact . . . some of the cross-country travels were removed or spliced together."[3] Such splicings, however, could have helped to achieve the novel's balanced four-part structure; each contains a story-within-a-story that reinforces the predominant impression left by the work as a whole, as summed up in the brief fifth part. If the original version of the text was, like some of Kerouac's others, analogous to a jazz improvisation, Cowley's "big changes" may have turned *On the Road* into a symphonic work, in which the patterns of the four movements are repetitive and incremental rather than varied in temper as they are in the traditional musical form of the symphony.

Before looking closely at the structure of the novel, however, we must consider what—from a chronological point of view—is included, and what is left out. Even though the account of Kerouac's cross-country junkets may have been streamlined, the order of events in the novel still corresponds closely enough to the order of similar events in the author's life to make it possible to date them with some precision. The narrative begins when Sal Paradise (based on Kerouac himself) meets Dean Moriarity (based on Neal Cassady) for the first time around Christmas 1946 in New York City, and it ends shortly after Sal gets back to New York after a devastating trip to Mexico City with Dean in October 1950. The time spanned is thus just slightly less than four years, but the events depicted in the novel occur within just twenty-four months. Part 1 parallels Kerouac's first long junket into the West between December 1946 and October 1947. Of the next thirteen months, however, Sal says only, "It was over a year before I saw Dean again. I stayed home all that time, finished my book and began going to school on the GI Bill of Rights."[4] The action does not resume until December 1948, and part 2 uses events only from that month and January 1949. After a brief break, the action resumes in part 3 in April 1949 and continues until July. There follows another long break until March 1950, when Sal, like Kerouac having just sold his first novel, sets off on the road on his own–for the first time without Dean.

The novel opens with the curt announcement that Sal first met Dean not long after he had split up with his wife and suffered a serious illness, but he does not want to talk about these events, which are part of a dead past. "With the coming of Dean Moriarity," he announces, "began the part of my life you could call my life on the road" (5). It is this life, and only this life, with which the novel is concerned. It begins with a major turning-point in the narrator's life, and the reader is given few glimpses into what has gone before. The novel ends almost four years later with Sal's split-up with Dean, another major turning point in his life, and we have little hint of what comes afterwards. (It is important to note here that Kerouac did continue seeing Neal Cassady after the separation dramatized in the novel in order to emphasize that we should always remember that *On the Road,* no matter how much autobiographical material it draws upon, is a self-contained picaresque tale that needs to be interpreted on its own terms and not viewed as a literal record of the Kerouac-Cassady relationship.)

Since Sal's connection with Dean begins after the breakup of a marriage and depicts the finally unsuccessful effort to establish an intimate bond with another man, some readers have been tempted to interpret the work in homosexual terms—a temptation encouraged by Neal Cassady's known bisexual practices (including a short-lived relationship with Allen Ginsberg) and Kerouac's own ambiguous sexuality. Suspicion is also supported by the almost too strident fag-bashing tone that Sal adopts whenever he speaks about "fairies" in the book. A preoccupation with this thesis, however, leads to a confusion between fiction and possible reality that distracts attention from the novel itself. Sal Paradise's emphasis throughout his narrative is upon the quest not for a lover, but for a brother, reflecting Kerouac's own effort to find a replacement for his dead brother Gerard, with whom as a child he had identified himself. Cassady also closely resembles the fictional figure of brother Joe Martin in *The Town and the City,* with whom Peter Martin had shared a bedroom as a child.

At the emotional climax of the novel in part 3, when Dean is beginning to be denounced and shunned by former friends and even relatives, Sal's defense of him has religious rather than sexual overtones. When Galatea Dunkel charges that Dean has "done so many awful things I don't know what to say to you," Sal experiences the revelation that has most upset many of the commentators already appalled by the behavior of the characters in the novel—"Dean, by virtue of his enormous series of sins, was becoming the Idiot, the Imbecile, the Saint of the lot. . . . That's what Dean was, the HOLY GOOF" (160–61).

Sal has earlier realized that the relationship described in the novel is reaching its crisis: "It was probably the pivotal point of our friendship when he realized I had actually spent some hours thinking about him and his troubles" (156), and they resolve to go to Italy. The exact nature of the relationship as Sal conceives it is brought out when Sal is questioned by two college boys who are frightened by Dean's wild driving. When they ask if he is Sal's brother, Sal replies, "He's mad . . . and yes, he's my brother" (187).

Despite Sal's "amazed" attention to Dean's "enormous dangle" in a nude drawing of Dean by his girl friend (38), a serious objection to viewing Sal's attachment to Dean as a search for a substitute spouse rather than a putative brother is the very structure of the story. As we have seen, Dean is a part of Sal's life only when they are on the road; almost half of the elapsed time, however, Sal is back home in New York, working, writing, living with his aunt, completing his novel and eventually selling it. Sal is thus a split character, although in *On the Road,* Kerouac has combined the parts of a personality divided in *The Town and the City* between two brothers into a single figure who moves back and forth between two quite different lives. Only the most fleeting references are made, however, to the life he lives off the road; the novel is intensely focused on only the half of his life that he lives on the road where Dean serves as his guide and model, although he never becomes a full-time partner in both halves of Sal's divided life.

Not much attention has been paid in criticism of the novel to the fact that it is focused solely on half of Sal's life, although this focusing needs to be taken into account in speculating about the audience's favorable reaction to the work. The life on the road that is depicted is, of course, the exciting part of Sal's life. Living at home, being cared for by one's aunt, working on a novel, even achieving commercial success is not exciting, so that in this novel when the narrator skips over half his life hardly anyone notices.

By thus intensely focusing the story—a focusing that must have been strengthened by Malcolm Cowley's suggested revisions, even if in accord with Kerouac's original intentions—Kerouac could be employing Poe's theories about narrative construction explained in his review of Hawthorne's *Twice-Told Tales.* In this landmark statement, Poe explains that when a skillful literary artist ideally constructs a tale "he has not fashioned his thoughts to accommodate his incidents, but having conceived, with deliberate care, a certain unique or single *effect* to be wrought out, he then invents such incidents—he then combines such events as may best aid him" to the "outbringing" of this preconceived effect, so that "during the hour of perusal the soul of the reader is at the writer's control."

Kerouac's other writings, neither the diffuse and rambling *The Town and the City* nor his later strivings for spontaneity, followed no such practice; but *On the Road* illustrates (though probably not deliberately) Poe's principles, especially in putting the soul of the reader at the writer's control during the hour of perusal.

The novel can be discussed in terms of Poe's theory (despite Poe's own distrust of such an extended form) because each of the four major sections can be read as an individual tale at a single sitting. The second, third, and fourth parts are remarkably comparable in length, and the first is substantially longer only because it contains a section that sharply contrasts with the episodes concerning Sal and Dean and that has no counterpart in the succeeding sections. Otherwise all four parts are remarkably similar in structure, each leading to the same kind of conclusion, one that serves to foreshadow and reinforce the conclusion of the whole tale in the brief fifth section.

The Parts and the Whole

Each of the four major parts of the novel describes one of Sal's road trips, reflecting Kerouac's own major ventures between 1946 and 1950. Each of these parts follows a remarkably similar pattern leading to identical conclusions. Each begins with Sal tired and depressed and seeking an escape from a troublesome or boring situation in his "other life." He at first takes to the road slowly and cautiously, but as he gains confidence and becomes energized by this new life, the action accelerates until it reaches a high point at which a disappointing experience causes things to fall to pieces, and Sal returns home (often slinking there) dejected and depressed again.

In part 1, Sal meets Dean in December 1946, but it is the following July before he has saved enough money to venture out on the road. His initial attempts at hitchhiking are futile, and he has to take a bus to Chicago. On his way to Denver, however, he begins to pick up the beat of life on the road. He takes the bus again to San Francisco, where instead of enjoying life as he has expected he ends up as a security guard in a construction camp with a tyrannous chief. This experience leads him to conclude that "this is the story of America. Everybody's doing what they think they're supposed to do" (57). Things have not worked out at all, and he laments how different the reality has proved from what he had envisioned: "Here I was at the end of America—and now there was nowhere to go but back" (66).

On this trip, however, a determination to go to Los Angeles leads Sal into the one genuinely promising relationship that he develops.

He meets a Mexican girl named Terry on a bus and has his only rewarding romantic relationship with a woman with her. They spend only fifteen days together, however, because he is broke. She is supposed to follow him to New York, but Sal comments with sad finality, "We both knew she wouldn't make it." (85). Why he fails to pursue the relationship is not revealed, however, until much later in the book, when, mooning in Denver's colored section, he wishes that he belonged to one of the oppressed but happy minorities and was anything but what he was "so drearily, a 'white man' disillusioned." In one of the most startling and surprising statements in the novel, he blurts out, "All my life I'd had white ambitions; that was why I'd abandoned a good woman like Terry" (148).

More than a year passes before Dean turns up again at the start of part 2 to help Sal move his mother's furniture to his sister's house in North Carolina. Then Sal wants to set off on one more "magnificent" trip to the West Coast before he returns to school in the spring. After troubles with a "Victorian police force," the travelers visit Old Bull Lee (based on William Burroughs) near New Orleans, where he is raising marijuana; but at the last minute Dean antagonizes Old Bull by using his con man tactics to try to borrow money. Finances become increasingly difficult, but when the travelers at last reach the Golden Gate, Dean dumps Sal and Marylou (the girl that Dean had brought East with him); and Sal realizes "what a whore she was" (142). The deflating climax comes, however, when Dean tries to make some money selling a new kind of pressure cooker at home demonstrations. One morning Sal sees Dean standing naked by the window and observes that "he looked like someday he'd be the pagan mayor of San Francisco," but in the judgment that marks the climax of the novel and begins an increasingly depressing picture of the life on the road, Sal observes, "But his energies ran out" (145). Life on the road has been built on "a hurricane of energy," but people have limitations that make it impossible to sustain this life of irresponsible kicks. Sal has become tired of the whole business and remains in California only until a compensation check arrives that enables him to take the bus back home again. "What I accomplished by coming to Frisco I don't know," he observes. As he parts with Dean and Marylou, he laments, "We were all thinking we'd never see one another again and we didn't care" (147).

By spring, however, he has saved a few dollars and takes off again for Denver, thinking of settling there. But he finds, as he reflects on his "white ambitions" that it is too late: "always it had been college, big-time, sober-faced; no boyish, human joy. . . . All I did was die" (149). When a rich girl gives him a hundred dollars, he is drawn back to San Francisco, where Dean greets him naked in the doorway (150). (Sal's frequent emphasis on Dean's nakedness also suggests a sexual preoccupation, but Sal never admits any physical response. The nakedness seems rather to symbolize Sal's conception of Dean as a kind of primitive force, unrestrained by any social institutions, until his energies give out.) After hearing Dean's tales of woe about his tangled domestic affairs, Sal offers to take the responsibility for supporting them both and proposes the trip to Italy. They set off for the East on a terrifying drive in a car obtained from an agency that provides drivers for other people's vehicles.

Along the way, Sal becomes increasingly defensive as Dean is attacked by family and friends, but even he is beginning to lose faith in the lure of the endless road: "I was beginning to cross and recross towns in America as though I was a traveling salesman—raggedy travelings, bad stock, rotten beans in the bottom of my bag of tricks, nobody buying" (202). In New York, the patient aunt into whom Kerouac has transformed his mother for this tale allows Dean to stay only a few days. Although Dean and Sal agree to remain friends forever, within a few days Dean is involved with still another woman and a few months later, he has four children on his hands, two illegitimate. "So we didn't go to Italy," Sal ends this installment in curt disgruntlement.

Selling his novel, however, enables him to take to the road with regenerated enthusiasm in the spring of 1950, as in part 4 for the first time he leaves Dean behind and sets off on his own. Dean turns up, however, on his way to Mexico to get a divorce, and Sal is suddenly aglow in anticipation of the unimaginable prospects of "the most fabulous" trip of all. As they enter Mexico, Dean enthuses, "Now, Sal, we're leaving everything behind us and entering a new and unknown phase of things. All the years and troubles and kicks—and now this!" (226), but *this* turns out to be only more of the same old frustration and disillusionment. After some nights of innocent fun, Sal comes down with a bad fever, and Dean, who has gotten his divorce, deserts Sal, telling him only, "Gotta get back to my life" (248). When Sal recovers, he realizes "what a rat" Dean was (249); but recognizing the hopeless complexity of Dean's life, he promises the absent Dean to say nothing.

This concluding disillusionment with Dean and the life he promises and Sal's resignation should not come, however, as a surprise to the careful reader. Very early in the book Sal acknowledged that Dean is a con man, but justifies his behavior on the grounds that "he was only conning because he wanted so much to live and to get involved with people who would otherwise pay no attention to him. He was conning me and I knew it . . . and he knew I knew (this has been the basis of our relationship)" (8). Sal apparently hopes that out of his bag of tricks, Dean might generate energies that would lead to a magnificent life on the road. His hopes are dashed, however, when Dean's energies run out in San Francisco; he will never become the "pagan mayor" who will generate a new order of things. From this point forward, despite some desperate efforts on Sal's part to sustain the relationship, it gradually deteriorates until Dean walks out on Sal in Mexico City, unable to accept responsibility that will interfere with his uncontrollable impulses.

Those who have denounced *On the Road* as promoting the adoption of life on the road have certainly failed to notice two passages late in the novel that reflect Sal's state of mind before he is lured into the final disastrous adventure.

Looking over some photographs of friends just before Sal sets off on the last trip by himself, he muses: "I realized these were all the snapshots which our children would look at someday with wonder, thinking their parents had lived smooth, well-ordered, stabilized-within-the-photo lives and got up in the morning to walk proudly on the sidewalks of life, never dreaming the raggedy madness and riot of our actual lives, our actual night, the hell of it, the senseless nightmare road. All of it inside endless and beginningless emptiness" (208). Just before this he has told the man who had been the embodiment of the life on the road, "All I hope, Dean, is someday we'll be able to live on the same street with our families and get to be a couple of oldtimers together" (207). No wonder that the novel ends with Sal sitting "on the old broken-down river pier watching the long, long skies over New Jersey" (as anyone who has seen this particular Hudson riverscape knows, it is one of the most dismal prospects anywhere), musing, as the sun goes down, that "nobody knows what's going to happen to anybody besides the forlorn rags of growing old" (254).

Just prior to these lines, Kerouac provides one of the most brilliant images anywhere in his fiction to convey the state of mind of his nar-

rator. Back in New York, his novel published, Sal is riding to a Duke
Ellington concert at the Metropolitan Opera House with an old friend
who has had handpainted for the occasion one of those garish early
1950s ties that Frederic Wakeman satirizes in *The Hucksters*, "on it
was painted a replica of the concert tickets, and the names Sal and
Laura and Remi and Vicki, the girl, together with a series of sad
jokes and some of his favorite sayings such as 'You can't teach the old
maestro a new tune' " (253). Dean asks for a ride, but Remi—Sal's
host—refuses, so that Sal can only sit in the back seat of a bookie's
Cadillac and wave through the window to Dean.

The image perfectly encapsulates the whole drift of the novel: Sal,
despite his efforts to break out, is left behind glass, the captive of his
"white ambitions," unable to communicate with Dean, who is left
behind to shiver in the New York cold. Sal has been on the road, but
never *of* the road. After each adventure, he has withdrawn to a protected environment. Dean has repeatedly tempted him out before, but
fails to do so on this final occasion.

To call *On the Road*, a bildungsroman, a novel of education, is a
misapplication of the term; for in such a novel the protagonist is substantially changed by his experiences, but Sal Paradise never changes.
He is rather simply confirmed in the identity that he possessed before
the beginning of the novel. Sal has recognized Dean as a confidence
man from the beginning of their association, but he has allowed himself at times to be hypnotized by Dean's energies, which promise a
magical new world. When these energies run out, Sal wakes up and
finds himself back in the same old world that he left, neither happy
nor comfortable, but captive to the materialistic world of bad taste
and conspicuous consumption epitomized by the final Cadillac ride.
He sees no future, but "the forlorn rags of growing old."

The Appeal of *On the Road*

On the Road is thus not, except at occasional moments early in each
of its four major parts, a carefree, upbeat promotion of an irresponsible life on the road that presents a formidable threat to the traditional
American way of life; rather it is a distinctly downbeat work, with a
conclusion in which the narrator is distinctly "beat" in the com-
monest sense of the word meaning something battered by the world
(and *beat* is most frequently used in this sense in this novel). The conclusion is foreshadowed and reinforced by the movement of each of

the four major parts from beginnings full of happy anticipations through periods of frenzied excitement to depressing conclusions portraying the characters' frustration and exhaustion.

What does an audience find appealing about such a work? Despite harsh attacks by establishment critics, the work was an immediate success, and it has remained steadily in print, attracting a sizeable cult following that has been regularly renewed, especially among high school and college readers. It continues to be attacked, often quite virulently, but usually by people who do not appear to have read the novel itself but to have been influenced by media stereotypes of the Beat Generation and the more sensational passages from Allen Ginsberg's poem *Howl*. Certainly it is not a novel that preaches the benefits of rebellion any more than is J. D. Salinger's *Catcher in the Rye*.

What the novel communicates, in fact, is much like Holden Caulfield's advice to his readers after he has spent a night trying to sleep on a bench in Grand Central Station, "Don't ever try it. I mean it. It'll depress you." Certainly an attempt to duplicate the ironically named Sal Paradise's life on the road would prove equally depressing. Far from inciting the reader to hit the road, *On the Road* proves a traditional cautionary tale, warning readers about the sorry nature of the world. It promises the reader nothing but disappointment and disillusionment.

Although this is not the way the novel has usually been described, it is supported by a careful analysis of the narrative, and it not only best suits the work, but is in keeping with what might be anticipated from the work of a basically conservative young person as he faces a critical test as to which part of his divided personality will dominate his life. Can he really overcome his "white ambitions" to adopt a spontaneous, irresponsible way of life? We should not be surprised after reading *On the Road* that its author would subsequently, in an article entitled "After Me, the Deluge," reveal that he feels lost in contemporary America, fulminate against Jerry Rubin, Abbie Hoffman, Ken Kesey, Timothy Leary, and his former close friend Allen Ginsberg, and finally refuse to accept any responsibility for the kind of youth culture that others blame him for promoting.[5]

Perhaps Kerouac's own expectations are best summed up in Sal Paradise's reflection before the second and shortest of his trips, "What I wanted was to take one more magnificent trip to the West Coast and get back in time for the spring semester in school" (107)—a manifestation of the urge that drives thousands of college students every spring to Daytona Beach and Fort Lauderdale. What he is telling readers is that such junkets promise to be great fun, but prove exhausting and disappointing. Hopeful young readers are likely, however, to be inclined to do what he himself did rather than what he tells them to do. *On the Road* is surely a novel that has been more enthusiastically than carefully read, so that professional busybodies are probably correct in feeling that it might foster delinquent impulses, but only because they have missed the point themselves. A familiar case of the blind presuming to lead the blind.

The novel cannot be dismissed as simply exciting fare for careless readers. Perhaps even only unconsciously, many readers are likely to be affected by the underlying despair that the novel expresses. The view that Sal finally espouses as he sits forlornly watching the coming of night and its symbolic anticipation of growing old is that people's energies are not equal to the demands that youth greedily imposes upon them. Driving fast and dangerously is an exhilarating experience for a while, but people, like cars, finally run out of gas. *On the Road* suggests that maturity offers no rewards; there is only, after the excitement of youth, "the forlorn rags of growing old." What the novel ultimately fosters is not rebellion, but sullen resignation.

It may be, of course, the very defeatist aspects of the conclusion that have most bothered high-minded attackers who are still guided (or misguided) by Longfellow's injunction that "life is earnest, life is real." If Kerouac's novel serves to stimulate any sensibility, it is not that of an ebullient youth cult, but a world-weariness that harks back to the French decadents of the fin de siècle, as is evidenced also by Kerouac's fondness for Rimbaud.

On the Road is, thus, ultimately a defeatist book, but this very quality may account for its appeal. Americans are not really educated to be winners, and few of them know how to win gracefully. Most, especially of Kerouac's generation that grew up during the Depression, expect to lose and to be taken in by confidence men. It remains to be seen whether the new generation of "Yuppies" are to enjoy a basically different experience, but for those who have been for thirty years the enthusiastic readers of the book its underlying appeal may be that it does indeed really show things as they are—and shows that they are not very good.

Although the language and the settings are new, *On the Road* is a traditional tale of youth's disillusionment, perhaps closest in the American tradition to Fitzgerald's *The Great Gatsby*. What was distinctly new and different about the book, however, was that the disenchantment, traditionally regarded as the preserve of the rich, was transferred here not to poor, honest working people—as in the writings of Dreiser and the proletarians—but to questionable bohemians operating on the margins of society.

Kerouac's work may have gone unpublished as long as it did because most of the reputable American publishers regard themselves as refined and genteel caterers to a refined and genteel audience. They would have been uneasy about introducing into the homes of their customers ruffians whom one would certainly avoid in public. Publishers tend, until pressed by powerful forces of public opinion, to print what they think readers ought to want to read; so they find it difficult to recognize changes occurring in the audience or new voices that might appeal to a changed audience, even when those voices are saying the same things as the established literati but not in the expected way.

Chapter Four
Off the Track

The Subterraneans (1953, 1958)

While *The Subterraneans* is usually looked upon as part of the Duluoz Legend, it would take very extensive revision to fit this nearly hysterical tale into the whole panoramic work.[1] In the first place, the name used here for Kerouac's alter ego, Leo Percepied, occurs only in this brief novel and was apparently not a substitution required by cautious publishers. It is difficult, therefore, to ignore the symbolic implications of the name, which could be translated "Lion with a Pierced-Foot," suggesting some kind of primitive jungle king disabled by a crippling wound or with an Achilles' heel. Although the novel has been praised by those close to Kerouac for its verisimilitude, its credibility is immediately suspect because of the fact that, although it parallels events that took place in New York's Greenwich Village during the summer of 1953, the novel is set in San Francisco.

It is also entirely different in tone from any of the novels in which Kerouac is transformed into Ti Jean Duluoz. It is the most sexually specific of any of Kerouac's works, so that is is understandable why he asked his mother not to look at it. Leo Percepied is much closer to John Clellan Holmes's Gene Pasternak in *Go*, an irresponsible womanizer, than any other of Kerouac's avatars in his own fiction.

The novel has been praised by Kerouacophiles as one of the best illustrations of his technique of "sketching"; detailed study of the complex structures of some of the sentences—especially as they are analogous to the techniques of jazz improvisation praised in the novel—serve to document Kerouac's often elusive concept of "spontaneous prose," so that the novel strikes one as more an exercise in style than a contemplated contribution to a Legend covering a lifetime. Even such a novel, however, is more than an exercise in style; when one breaks the almost hypnotic spell that Kerouac in his best improvisatory moments creates with a torrent of words, and seeks out the underlying theme that is obscured by the artful variations, one discovers that this tale is a nasty bit of business indeed.

Apparently few readers have taken a close, critical look at the novel, or else by now it would have become a glaring example for antiracist and feminist critics of the attitudes they decry in American culture and its mainstream literary tradition. Far more than television's famous bigot Archie Bunker, Leo Percepied is the fictional embodiment of the woman-degrading, male chauvinist, racist, and homophobic attitudes that have engendered some of the ugliest controversies in the United States since World War II.

Ostensibly this is the story of a two-month love affair between Percepied and a half-black, half-Indian outcast girl named in the novel Mardou Fox (for understandable reasons, the model for this character has never permitted herself to be identified); but, despite the inclusion of one of the grossest descriptions of sexual relations to be found even in recent sensational literature, climaxing the description of "the precious good moments" that the couple has enjoyed,[2] the emphasis is on the bad times ("I have a list of bad times"—Percepied interjects parenthetically into this account—"to make the good times, the times I was good to her and like I should be, to make it sick.")

This negative emphasis is scarcely surprising in the account of an affair that begins with Percepied's avowing on first seeing Mardou, "By God, I've got to get *involved* with that *little* woman" (10, italics mine), a sentiment exactly in keeping with his description of himself as "crudely malely sexual and cannot help myself and have lecherous and so on propensities." Although some readers may be outraged by the universalizing "as almost all my male readers are no doubt the same" (11) that concludes this "confession," at least we are informed about the stereotypes that shape the narrator's thinking about women and about other men and their interrelationships, so that we proceed at our own risk. We should scarcely later be surprised that even three weeks before the end of this affair, which lasts only two months, Percepied is plotting to end it. He never specifies his reasons for this quick change, although they are implied through the principal events of the story. Percepied several times expresses regret about the actions—admittedly his own—that end the affair; at one point he even utters the incredible aside that "poverty would have saved this romance," in spite of the fact that both he and Mardou are totally broke throughout.

The principal reason for its inevitable outcome has nothing to do with finances, but is the product of his condescending attitudes towards Mardou, whom he refers to as a "poor subterranean beat Negro girl with no clothes on her back worth a twopenny" (104). In one of the most incredibly patronizing remarks one is likely to encounter in literature, Percepied also reports that when they try to communicate with each other telepathically, he undermines the experiment through his "fear of communicating WHITE images to her . . . for fear she'll be (in her fun) reminded of our racial difference, at that time making me feel guilty, now I realize it was love's gentility on my part—Lord" (83). One example suffices to illustrate his running comments about Mardou's being "unable to bear the polite conversation" of his friends, "the likes of which," he has earlier assured us, "cannot be surpassed anywhere in the world" (113, 103).

Reading these remarks out of context one would suppose that they were intended sarcastically, but the whole slant of the novel is toward making one sympathize with the suffering Leo, as evidently many readers have. Behind the intellectual snobbery here lie "the white ambitions" that Sal Paradise in *On the Road* had blamed for the breakup of his genuinely affectionate relationship with the Mexican girl Terry. Early in *The Subterraneans,* Percepied, again universalizing himself, explains to "all lover readers who've suffered pangs," the principal sources of his doubts about the relationship—"doubts, therefore, of, well, Mardou's Negro, naturally not only my mother but my sister whom I may have to live with some day and her husband a Southerner and everybody concerned would be mortified to hell and have nothing to do with us—like it would preclude completely the possibility of living in the South" (56). When Mardou is afraid to go into a white bar with him, he tries to console her with the thought that some day, "in fact baby I'll be a famous man and you'll be the dignified wife of a famous man so don't worry"; not surprisingly, she responds, "You don't understand" (81).

Indeed when the final breakup with Mardou comes as a result of Leo's petulant behavior, fancying himself "the only man in South City who ever walked from the neat suburban homes and went and hid by boxcars to think" the vision that cracks him up at last is of his mother, bending over him and saying in Quebecois, which he painstakingly translates for the reader after quoting the original, "Poor Little Leo . . . you suffer, men suffer so, you're all alone in the world I'll take care of you . . . my angel" (119).

The Subterraneans, thus, even more than *On the Road,* justifies John Updike's malicious parody of Kerouac's mother fixation.[3] In terms of the "Peter-Francis" split in Kerouac's personality, this is clearly one of "Peter's" works, which ends with the narrator's return after a brush with the strange and frightening to the comforts and security of home. In fact, from the point of view of exposing the author's rather than the narrator's psychology, the novel is of considerable interest as one in which we witness a transformation of Mr. Hyde back to Dr. Jekyll as homebody Peter worms his way out of an affair into which Francis, with his exotic tastes, has plunged him.

There is more to the breakup of the affair in *The Subterraneans*, however, than simply the overwhelming of a free spirit tempted to take dangerous chances by oedipal immaturity; an element missing from *On the Road*, in which "Peter" is suppressed until the end while "Francis" tells of his adventures, emerges here in the description of the kind of "tests" that Leo Percepied tries on Mardou Fox to determine her faithfulness.

When at one point Leo becomes jealous of a black man's attentions to Mardou, Adam Moorad, a character based on Allen Ginsberg, advises Leo, "If she should hear that you went out with a white girl to see if you could make it again she'd sure be flattered" (88), but the tests that Leo devises actually do not involve other women at all.

Early in the novel Leo admits that the "first foolish mistake in my life and love with Mardou" was refusing to go home with her after a party breaks up because he has been invited to stay and "study" the host's "pornographic (homo male sexual) pictures" (48), although he never explains the source of his interest in them. The two tests that he imposes upon Mardou, however, certainly involve homoeroticism. The first concerns a famous visiting novelist, Arial Lavalina, of whom Gore Vidal has admitted being the original. Leo describes Lavalina as being a "perfectly obvious homosexual"; yet he abandons Mardou to go spend the night at a hotel with the writer. His account of what transpired is ambiguous, as he acknowledges only that he woke up on a couch the next morning with the "horrible recognition" that he never did get to Mardou's and that he decided to apologize at once to Lavalina "for getting so drunk and acting in such a way to mislead him" (66). Vidal, however, insists elsewhere that on the occasion mirrored here, Kerouac did go to bed with him, a fact Kerouac later reluctantly acknowledged.[4]

The second test involves Leo's attentions to a "beautiful faun boy," who follows a party of subterraneans from bar to bar, until Mardou finally yells at Leo, "It's him or me goddamit" (67) and leaves still yelling, "We're through," though Leo refuses to believe it. Later Leo is accused by Frank Carmody (apparently based on William Burroughs) of getting "a reputation on the Beach as a big fag tugging at the shirts of well-known punks" (74), and Leo and Mardou attend a party arranged by a friend with Leo's "acquiescence," at which the other guests "were just boys and all queer" (80). Homosexual jokes are scattered throughout the text, and much of the action takes place in a deteriorating lesbian bar.

Friends have circulated stories about Kerouac's involvement in homosexual activities, but nowhere else in his writing is such an emphasis placed on testing a female lover by attentions not to other women, but to gay men. It is dangerous here, as elsewhere, to assume that the narrator is a faithful reproduction of the author; but a serious question of literary intentions is raised when an infatuation (and that is all that the love affair here can really be called) is relatively quickly overcome not by the attraction of competing women but by repeated involvement with homosexual men. The question is especially intriguing in a novel that portrays the overwhelming of the adventurous, alienated "Francis" by conservative homebody "Peter."

Since Leo never develops any deep relationship, however, with any of the gay characters he meets, we must consider the possibility that his real interest is in avoiding any kind of commitments at all because of his primary interest in what he describes as his "all consuming work" (64). He continually places his emphasis upon the importance of his "work" (64); indeed the novel ends, not with Leo's redeeming vision of his mother, but with his acknowledgment that having lost Mardou's love, he went home to "write this book" (126).

Ann Charters seems completely justified in her conclusion that "Kerouac's pride in tossing *The Subterraneans* off in three nights gave him more lasting satisfaction than anything that happened between him and the girl that summer. . . . He never got that deeply emotionally involved."[5] This observation, however, prompts the question of whether he ever got deeply emotionally involved with anyone except his mother. The tests that he has Leo impose upon Mardou can be interpreted as aimed at determining whether she was going to insist that his relationship with her be taken more seriously than his relationships with his gay bar companions. In any event *The Subterraneans* can only finally be satisfactorily interpreted as the portrait of an individual who uses other people simply as grist for the machinations of his own imagination. No wonder when after Kerouac's death Charters asked the girl who was the original of Mardou how she felt about what happened, she only shrugged—"none of it was important to her."[6] The novel portrays a few days' dalliance in the life of a totally narcissistic person, but there is no evidence that the author has any insight into the story that he is telling. Like *On the Road, The Subterraneans* cannot be called a *Bildungsroman* because the narrator has learned nothing. It is a portait of a young prig from whom the author has not ironically distanced himself.

The Dharma Bums (1957, 1958)

While *The Dharma Bums* unquestionably makes a contribution toward filling an important gap in the Duluoz Legend by supplying Kerouac's only account based on some important months before the publication of *On the Road,* it suffers from having been hurriedly written on commission and never revised or rewritten. The tentativeness of the novel is indicated by Kerouac's using here, for the only time in a published work, the name Ray Smith for his alter ego; although he had used the same name in one of the early, unfinished versions of *On the Road,* so that it is associated with uncompleted efforts to find himself. His fuller treatment in *Desolation Angels* of the narrator's final days as a fire watcher on Desolation Mountain and of what followed after he came down also suggest what Kerouac might finally make of the material from this period. As it stands, the novel can only be regarded as the potboiler that Kerouac himself considered it,[7] even though it has been one of his most popular novels after *On the Road.* Certainly it is one of his most poorly structured works.

The problem with the novel is that Allen Ginsberg was right when, after a sympathetic review in the *Village Voice,* he privately advised Kerouac to stop writing "travelogues."[8] Although the book is not divided into sections, it, like *On the Road,* joins together four separate episodes. Though this time the action is continuous, the episodes are not paralleled by any climactic dramatic structure that gives the narrative shape as a whole. The trouble does not seem to have been that Kerouac could not find a unifying device, but that he seems not to have cared about finding one. He was simply in a hurry to get it done. The book was written about the period when Buddhist influences in his life were at their height and when the two conflicting natures in his personality seemed to have most nearly reached resolution with the exotic, aesthetic Francis in control and farmboy Peter emerging only occasionally to introduce Christian pieties.

What unity the novel has derives from its fictionalizing the months of Kerouac's most intense association with Gary Snyder, who here appears in the person of Japhy Ryder. Ryder is present only in the first and third episodes, but the Buddhist leanings that provided his finally unstable link with Kerouac color the whole narrative.

The first section, which runs more than one-third of the length (70 of 187 pages), begins with the famous description of the beginnings of the San Francisco Poetry Renaissance on 13 October 1955 with Allen Ginsberg's reading of *Howl* for the first time at the Six Gallery; but consists mostly of a minutely detailed account of Kerouac's first mountain climbing expedition with Snyder and John Montgomery (Henry Morley in the text) on the California Matterhorn.[9] Ray Smith then takes off on a transcontinental journey, accomplished mostly through the courtesy of a truckdriver who befriends him near Calexico on the Mexican border and transports him to Ohio. Smith then travels on to North Carolina to spend the winter and early spring with his mother, sister, and brother-in-law.

When things become tense there, especially after his mother leaves, because he spends his time in the woods meditating while the others work, Smith takes off again for the West Coast by bus. Here he spends an idyllic time, described in another seventy pages, in a cabin in Marin County with Japhy Ryder before he takes off on a freighter for another stay in Japan.

Smith then goes to the state of Washington to spend the summer as a fire watcher in the mountains; but this episode, toward which the whole book has apparently been moving, is surprisingly thin, running only twenty-two pages, little more than ten percent of the whole text, most of which is taken up with somewhat tedious details of his preparations for the actual months of loneliness. Although we learn a great deal about Smith's meditations in North Carolina, we learn little about the nature of his experiences alone in the cabin on the mountain. The narrative ends abruptly with his going on "down the trail back to this world." While this ending is considerably more upbeat than that of *On the Road,* it conveys little sense of just what the whole year's experiences have added up to and accentuates the "travelogue" aspects of a book that is probably of greatest interest to those intrigued by Smith and Ryder's inconclusive palaverings about Buddhist theory and practice.

The action is episodic in the most negative sense of that term, for there is no cumulative movement toward what Poe called the outbringing of a "preconceived effect." Long passages of apparently unedited conversation alternate with moments of unassimilated violence. Kerouac could have benefited from contemplating Poe's strictures about the poem in "The Philosophy of Composition": "Had I been able, in the subsequent composition, to construct more vigorous stanzas, I should, without scruple, have purposely enfeebled them so as not to interfere with the climacteric effect."

A striking example of the inclusion of material with momentary shock value that is unwarranted by its contribution to any thematic pattern is the digressive introduction of the suicide of Rosie, the latest girl friend of Cody Pomeroy (based on Neal Cassady). Smith's only reaction to this sensational news is, "if she had only listened to me." It is followed by his decision to hit the road again, with the observation that "Rosie was a flower we let wither."[10] The incident is quickly passed over without being integated into any overall story line. Even Cody plays such a peripheral role in this story that it would have been better to omit his affairs altogether than to introduce them and then fail to integrate them into the action.

The excuse for mentioning Rosie's suicide cannot be that Kerouac attempted to mention everything that he was involved in during the period because, comparing the novel with information from other sources, we know that he did omit or downplay episodes that he might not have wanted to recall. He makes no attribution to Ray Smith during this period, for example, of *The Scripture of the Golden Eternity,* a Buddhist tract that Kerouac himself wrote at Gary Snyder's behest, since by the time he compiled the novel he was beginning to lose his interest in the subject, as he explains himself near the beginning of the novel: "I was very devout in those days and was practicing my religious devotions almost to perfection. Since then I've become a little hypocritical about my lip-service and a little tired and cynical" (6). Since we know that by 1960 Kerouac had become somewhat flippant about the whole Buddhist venture, the novel may not shed as much light as it could on the period when he was still enthusiastic about creating a kind of society from which he withdrew during the 1960s.

Probably the passage from the novel that has been most frequently taken out of context is Japhy Ryder's proclamation at a party after he returned from the mountain-climbing expedition:

I've been reading Whitman, know what he says, *Cheer up slaves, and horrify foreign despots,* he means that's the attitude for the Bard, the Zen Lunacy bard of old desert paths, see the whole thing is a world full of rucksack wanderers,

Dharma Bums refusing to subscribe to the general demand that they consume production and therefore have to work for the privilege of consuming
all that crap they don't really want anyway such as refrigerators, TV sets,
cars, at least new fancy cars, certain hair oils and deodorants and general junk
you always see a week later in the garbage anyway, all of them imprisoned
in a system of work, produce, consume, work, produce, consume, I see a
vision of a great rucksack revolution thousands or even millions of young
Americans wandering around with rucksacks, going up to mountains to
pray, making children laugh and old men glad, making young girls happy
and old girls happier. (78)

Significantly, this vision of an impending transformation in American life is assigned to Japhy (Gary Snyder). While it is reinforced on
a few other occasions, it is never developed to the extent that one
likes to recall it is in the novel.

Just before Japhy leaves for Japan, he does tell Ray that something
good is going to come out of their feelings about life: "You and I
ain't out to bust anybody's skull, or cut someone's throat in an economic way, we've dedicated ourselves to prayer for all sentient beings
and when we're strong enough we'll really be able to do it, too, like
the old saints" (166).

Ray himself also ventures into a much more genial, folksy version
of the venomous satire in Ginsberg's *Howl*, when he observes, riding
through Kansas City, "When I woke up in the morning, on Monday,
I looked out and saw all the eager young men in business suits going
to work in insurance offices hoping to be big Harry Trumans some
day" (104). At one point when Ray is depressed by the tyranny of the
authorities that threaten the rucksack revolution, he gives vent to an
almost incredible foreshadowing of the vision that will give force and
direction a few years later to Ken Kesey's *One Flew over the Cuckoo's
Nest*: "The only alternative to sleeping out, hopping freights, and doing what I wanted, I saw in a vision would be to just sit with a hundred other patients in front of a nice television set in a madhouse,
where we could be 'supervised' " (96).

These are only passing comments, however. Kerouac is not about
to depict or embrace any such confrontation as Kesey does. In his
"Biographical Resume" written the same year as *The Dharma Bums*,
he observed, "I am only a jolly storyteller and have nothing to do
with politics or schemes and my only plan is the old Chinese way of
the Tao: 'avoid the authorities.' "[11]

The irony about Kerouac's position is that there has been indeed a
rucksack revolution for which he has often been given credit, but in

which he played no part. Even if there has not been a transformation of American life on the scale that Japhy envisioned, one of the most profound long-term influences of the Beat Generation has been relaxing the tensions bred by the American "rat race" and helping to create, with the aid of meditation movements, a less disastrously competitive attitude in many young Americans. Ruckpacking has indeed become a widespread practice among American youth, which one can see today especially abroad, where thousands are enjoying a life that Kerouac himself found he could never master. Many have also been returning to the farms that Kerouac apostrophized but to which he never actually went back. Although *The Dharma Bums* has inspired many readers, it fails to develop a consistent enough vision to have become a prophetic guidebook. It is an unusual work from which readers appear to have derived more than the writer put into it, a work that is better remembered for its striking passages than digested as a whole.

Pic (1950 and 1969, 1971)

In 1971 after Kerouac's death, Grove Press published what many presumed to be his last novel. If *Pic* had been indeed the work of his final months, it would have represented a startling departure from the other writings of his last decade, for in it he abandons autobiographical materials to tell in first-person dialect the adventures of a naive but enterprising eleven-year-old North Carolina black boy, who is taken from his aunt's house by an older brother, with whom he travels to New York and California as the brother searches for work. Handling a difficult dialect with skill enough to be convincing, Kerouac seems to have been belatedly trying to make a fresh start as a fictionist by returning to the detached ironic mode of the Okinawa scene in *The Town and the City*.

Very little of *Pic*, however, appears to have been written in 1969. Although the unavailability of Kerouac's manuscripts makes certainty difficult, possibly only the final chapter was added to an earlier manuscript that Kerouac resurrected from his neatly kept files. The first hundred pages of the novelette can be identified as at least derived from one of Kerouac's early efforts to find a satisfactory form for the novel that would become *On the Road*.[12]

Dissatisfied with earlier efforts to tell the story in the third person, Kerouac, who had been visiting in North Carolina off and on since his sister's marriage in 1949, decided in 1950 to attempt a first-person narrative. For this purpose he contrived the character of eleven-year-old Pictorial Review Jackson, a black orphan whose hitherto uneventful life with his grandfather is disrupted when the old gentleman is taken to the hospital critically ill. Pic moves into the crowded home of his Aunt Gastonia, but encounters difficulties there, particularly with a vengeful Grandpa Jelkey, who had been blinded years earlier by Pic's fiery-tempered father. Pic's brother Slim turns up to take the boy away. When the Aunt refuses to surrender custody, Slim spirits Pic out of a bedroom window and rushes him to New York by bus.

All this activity was apparently intended as only the prologue to an account of the brothers' hitchhiking across the United States to seek a new life in California, where Slim's pregnant wife had already gone by bus. Only one chapter of the present text actually takes place on the road; but in this thirteenth chapter an unmistakable link with *On the Road* is established, because a brief account of the brothers' acquaintance with a mad old man headed for "Canady," whom they call "The Ghost of the Susquehanna," had already been published in quite similar form as the climax of Sal Paradise's unsettling experiences during his first round-trip across the continent in part 1 of *On the Road* (87–88). In *Pic,* Kerouac does not, however, have the narrator indulge in the pretentious meditation about the American wilderness that appears in *On the Road.* The material used in *Pic* seems to be the original version of an episode that was all Kerouac salvaged from the unfinished work when he returned to the project.

As Tim Hunt points out, Kerouac was still strongly under the influence of Mark Twain's *Adventures of Huckleberry Finn* when he conceived *Pic,* and had he continued the tale, the two black brothers would probably have developed even more strikingly into counterparts of Huck and Jim.[13] The best writing in the novelette occurs in the long chapter 10, during which it appears that Slim may get at least temporary work at his real trade of playing the horn in a jazz combo. Pic describes the effect of his brother's playing: "Oh, he talked and talked with that thing and told his story all over again, to me, to Sheila and ever'body. He jess had it in his heart what ever'body wanted in *their* hearts and they listened to him for some of it."[14] Perhaps it is significant that Pic at this time is "scarce eleven years old" (35), the same age that Kerouac was when he wrote his own first novel carefully modeled on *Huck Finn.*

Why Kerouac abandoned this narrative in 1950 is not clear, but

Hunt suspects that he became frustrated by the limitations of a child narrator.[15] In any event, Kerouac kept the uncompleted work in his files for two decades, and there is no reason to believe that he revised it substantially when he resurrected it at a time when he was in failing health and the family needed money desperately. The only certain example, therefore, of Kerouac's "last manner" is the tacked-on final chapter, in which he violates the original intention of the story by having Pic and Slim earn enough money in Pittsburgh to take the bus to California.

This sloppily written piece of something over a thousand words was reputedly composed to please Kerouac's mother.[16] In this sentimental episode, which harks back to the days when Kerouac admired William Saroyan, an Irish Catholic priest appears as a deus ex machina to bring the meandering tale to an abrupt and incredible conclusion when he discovers Pic's remarkable voice and pays the boy to sing in the church.

Several other quaint characters, including a mysterious woman, are introduced, but disappear without adding anything to the episode. Because of the contrast between the leisurely development of the scenes in North Carolina and the accounts of Pic's discovering the wonders of the life on the road, on the one hand, and the sudden, contrived ending, on the other, the novelette as a whole is a totally unsatisfying experience. It is doubtful that it would have been published at all if Kerouac's early death had not caused a stirring of new interest in his life. Even so it attracted little attention and few readers. Since no character in any way based on Kerouac himself appears in the short work, it has no place in the Duluoz Legend, although this last feeble effort to find a market for his work serves to reinforce our impression of what a downbeat ending the real life of Jean-Louis Lebris de Kerouac had.

Part Two

The Duluoz Legend

Chapter Five

Childhood—*Visions of Gerard* and *Doctor Sax*

Jean-Louis Lebris de Kerouac never carried out the intention he announced in his preface to *Big Sur*: "to collect all my work and re-insert my pantheon of uniform names," so that his legacy is a collection of fragments that we are left to reconcile with each other. Kerouac explains in *Vanity of Duluoz* that he came up with the idea of the Duluoz Legend in the purser's office on the *S.S. George Weems* in October or November 1943, after having read John Galsworthy's entire *Forsyte Saga*. He envisioned it as "a lifetime of writing about what I'd seen with my own eyes, told in my own words, according to the style I decided on at whether twenty-one years old or thirty or forty or whatever later age, and put . . . all together as a contemporary history record for future times to see what really happened and what people really thought."[1]

The name Duluoz was not new at that time. He had used it at least as early as the winter of 1942 when he began an uncompleted autobiographical novel called *Vanity of Duluoz*, although it did not appear in print until 1959 when *Doctor Sax* was published. "Duluoz" means "louse" in Quebecois; and Kerouac's use of it indicates a principal problem that plagued his attempts to shape an epic from his own experiences—a frequent whimsical undercutting of his heroic intentions by devices verging on self-parody.

The novels presenting the adventures and misadventures of Ti Jean Duluoz were neither written nor published in a sequence following the chronology of Kerouac's own life; but their arrangement in such an order, despite discontinuities resulting from Kerouac's changing styles, is the most satisfactory way to indicate how these works contribute to shaping a Legend.

Kerouac mentions in several places that Ti Jean's possibly earliest recollection was of when he was only a year old visiting with his mother a shoe repair shop with "shelves cluttered with dark shoes, innumerable battered shoes" on a "gray rainy day." Nothing is ever made dramatically of this possibly imaginary episode, but the comment that it inspires in *Visions of Gerard* sets the tone for much of the multivolumed Legend as a vision of "the great Gloom of the earth and the great Clutter of human life and the great Drizzly Dream of the dreary eternities." It concludes with a reflection on the "beatness" of the recollected scene that may be a memory "from some previous incarnation in St. Petersburg Russia or maybe the gluey ghees of dark fitful kitchens in Thibet ancient and long ago."[2]

Visions of Gerard (1925–26, 1956, 1963)

This keynote passage appears in the book that opens the Duluoz Legend by dealing with events that occurred during Duluoz's third and fourth year with the death of his sickly elder brother, the first really memorable experience in Ti Jean's life. (Gerard is one of the few characters to bear the same first name in both Kerouac's life and the Legend.)[3] The very short novel (fewer than one hundred fifty quite uncrowded pages interspersed with line drawings) has neither a plot nor any form of conventional suspense. We are told on the first page that Gerard will die and the narrative records his dying and its effects on others. "This gloomy book's foretold," Ti Jean informs us at one point (89).

Even in this recollection of childhood, however, we must be cautious—as with all contributions to the Legend—to bear in mind that it is not a literal record of Kerouac's past. As in any fiction shaped from the raw materials of the writer's experience, we are presented with an account of the way in which that writer would like us to perceive the experience.

The likelihood of literal accuracy is especially improbable with *Visions of Gerard*; for even though Kerouac could recall details from his past with such accuracy that friends called him "The Great Rememberer," his recollections of events that occurred when he was four years old are scarcely to be relied upon. What was Gerard really like? We shall never know, although other accounts, such as Charles Jarvis's,[4] generally agree with Kerouac's attribution to the child of a rare saintliness. What we perceive principally through the novel, however, is the image of a deceased sibling with whom the rememberer experienced a kind of absolute emotional identification that he had nurtured for three decades (it could scarcely have escaped Kerouac's notice that he composed his most Christian novel when he was an uncelebrated thirty-three years old). Although Kerouac referred only infrequently to Gerard in such later novels as *Vanity of Duluoz*, he does have Duluoz say in *Visions of Cody*, "I have not been the same since my brother Gerard died, when I was four" (359). The book is further distanced from reality because Kerouac was not interested in just chronicling his brother's short, painful life; he was concerned rather with creating an example of an ancient literary form rarely attempted today except by mystics like Thomas Merton, a saint's life—the purpose of which is not simply to justify the veneration of the subject but to provide the reader with a model for spiritual guidance.

The narrator begins by explaining that for the first four years of his life, he "was not Ti Jean Duluoz, I was Gerard, the world was his face, the flower of his face" (8). This floral image persists throughout the tale, as, for example, when Ti Jean speaks of Gerard as "a petallish thing" (85), a frail flower too soon withered by a sad world. With Gerard's death, Ti Jean loses his own prematurely precocious identity and much of what follows in his Legend relates to his efforts to replace his sanctifying identification with Gerard with some adequate substitute.

Slightly more than the first third of the book is devoted, as is appropriate in hagiography, to a recital of the special spiritual qualities of the subject, the "miracles" that justify his claims to eternal adoration. In view of Gerard's tender age and general immobility, these take mostly the form of his revulsion from the violence of this mortal sphere and his teachings of respect for all living things. When his cat eats a mouse that he has freed from a trap and is nursing back to health, he informs this "bad girl" who is the most faithful companion of his declining days, "We'll never go to heaven if we go on eating each other and destroying each other like that all the time!" (18), which leads Ti Jean to burst out that Gerard was "a soft tenderhearted angel the likes of which you'll never find again in science fictions of the future" (17).

This section of the novel is climaxed by an account of Gerard's vision on the last day that he is able to attend school. Accused by the sister-teacher in the Roman Catholic elementary school of dozing during the early morning catechism, Gerard astounds her and the class by announcing that he has seen the Virgin Mary. He has dreamed that he is sitting in a yard with his little brother when he is confronted by "a great White Virgin Mary with a flowing robe balloon-

ing partly in the wind and partly tucked in at the edges and held
aloft by swarms, countless swarms of grave bluebirds." She invites
him to follow her in his wagon, "the snow-white cart drawn by two
lambs" with two white pigeons "on each of his shoulders," beginning
an ascent to Heaven but just at this moment this "perfect ecstasy . . .
is rudely jolted by Sister Marie and he wakes to find himself in a
classroom" (65–66). The vision is premonitory, and it establishes a
special respect for Gerard that causes the nuns at the time of his actual death to hurry to his bedside to record last words that they never
disclose to his family.

After this episode, the narrative switches to an account of what else
is going on in town, especially to the brothers' financially troubled
father and his loutish associates, while Gerard is slowly fading away.
These fifty pages are not simply digressions; rather they represent a
necessary escape into more mundane matters of Gerard's bereaved
family now that his sad fate is sealed. Gerard does not fight against
the inevitable; from the beginning he has been ready to move to
heaven. His infantile perception of what is occurring, however, leads
Ti Jean to develop a philosophy of "our innocent mistaken earth"—
"God made us for His glory, not our own" (73), which will permeate
all the writings shaped predominantly by Kerouac's "Peter Martin"
voice.

Kerouac was never able to escape the concept instilled in him as a
child that he was only the plaything of a superior force and that human glory was illusory. The underlying struggle between this fatal-
ism instilled in him during his early years and his yearning to break
with an inhibiting past and strive for glory was one of the forces responsible for the Peter/Francis Martin split that was the basis of his
instability. Three-year-old Ti Jean could certainly not have articulated
the kind of identification with his brother that the thirty-three-year-
old writer attributed to his earlier self; its identification is part of
"Peter Martin's" recovery of a consoling past.

Gerard returns to take control of the book during the last thirty
pages as he is confined to the bedroom on what Ti Jean calls "the
little street that bears the great burden of Gerard's dying" (96). The
message that Gerard has for his little brother summarizes his earlier
teachings: "Always be careful not to hurt anyone—never get mad if
you can help it—I gave you a slap on the face the other day but I
didn't know it when I did it" (124).

This last sentence carries us back to one of the most curious episodes in the novel, Ti Jean's reconstruction of Gerard's first confession to a Roman Catholic priest, an event that the younger brother could neither have witnessed nor understood at the time. After pondering his sins, nine-year-old Gerard had made three childish confessions, all of which seem more likely to have been invented by the novelist inventorying his past than recalled from the conversation of the long-dead brother, even if they had been shared with such a young boy.

The least serious, which the priest dismisses, is that he told a nun that he had studied his catechism when he only recalled it from a previous occasion. Somewhat more serious is the slapping of his younger brother for destroying one of the fantastic constructions that Gerard had devised with his beloved Erector set, but the third, which most disturbs the priest, is Gerard's admission of his long inspection of a classmate's genitals at the urinal. The priest is relieved to hear that they had not actually touched each other; but the whole account, which the narrator lingers over in somewhat surprising detail, suggests a homoerotic curiosity and a condemnation of its sinfulness that may account for the ambiguousness Kerouac felt throughout his life in his relationships with other men to whom he felt a physical attraction that he could not admit had any sexual component.

Gerard's death makes one ponder what would have happened had he lived. This "what if" speculation is much more legitimate than most since Ti Jean himself brings up the matter: "And I wonder what Gerard would have done had he lived, sickly, artistic—But my good Jesus, with that holy face they'd have stumbled over one another to come and give him bread and breath—He left me his heart but not his tender countenance and sorrowful patience and kindly lights" (62).

How Ti Jean must have longed for others to give him "bread and breath" in his most beat moments, but, as this statement indicates, he believed that the better part of himself had died in childhood with Gerard, a self-concept that must be constantly borne in mind in evaluating the Duluoz Legend. That Charles Jarvis may be correct in asserting that "Gerard fashioned the great riffs that are Kerouac's novels,"[5] is supported by Ti Jean's account of his thoughts as he gazes at Gerard in his tiny coffin: "the whole reason why I ever wrote at all and drew breath to bite in vain with pen of ink, great gad with indefensible Usable pencil, because of Gerard, the idealism, Gerard the religious hero—"*Write in honor of his death*" (*Écrivez pour l'amour de son mort*) (as one would say, write for the love of God)" (132).

Considered as a saint's life, *Visions of Gerard* is a remarkable achievement for a twentieth-century writer generally regarded as an instigator of a counterculture. One can see through this portrait of Ti Jean Duluoz and his lost brother how strong a hold traditional culture had on the author. This is one of Kerouac's most readable books, and indeed it appears to be the only one that has commanded some success and respect in his home town. Its comparative obscurity must be charged principally to its being a work out of its time, an example of an old-fashioned genre written with a distinctly nineteenth-century sensibility. It is not a tale likely to appeal to the admirers of *On the Road* or *Visions of Cody*. It is in the literary traditions not only of the saint's tale, but also of Dickens's once popular accounts of the death of Little Nell in *The Old Curiosity Shop* and Paul Dombey in *Dombey and Son* and, very close to Kerouac's own home, Louisa May Alcott's rendering of the death of Beth in *Little Women*. It is the Peter Martin voice of Kerouac in its most pious and effective recapturing of the innocence of an earlier age.

Doctor Sax (1930–36, 1952, 1959)

The transition from *Visions of Gerard* to *Doctor Sax* is probably the most disorienting in the Kerouac canon. *Visions of Gerard* is the voice of "Peter Martin" producing Kerouac's easiest book to read; *Doctor Sax* is the voice of "Francis Martin" producing one of Kerouac's most difficult and puzzling works—an extremely important novel that holds a place analogous in his career to *A Portrait of the Artist as a Young Man* in James Joyce's.

The years immediately following Gerard's death are not accounted for anywhere in Kerouac's work.[6] Probably nothing happened to help him overcome the shock of the loss of his brother until he had matured sufficiently to begin to develop a sense of his individual identity. Also during his first years of school he faced the problem of replacing the Québécois that he had spoken with his family at home with the English his schooling in Lowell required, an effort that probably preoccupied him but that was likely to provide few novelistic situations.

Doctor Sax, which begins when the narrator is about eight years old, is Ti Jean's account of his discovery of the creative power within himself, a frightening, but ultimately liberating event. The book is puzzling, however, because Kerouac never has his narrator explain what he is doing in this work; he simply presents the reader with a strange variety of situations narrated in a mixture of styles with which the reader must come to terms in a fashion similar to the way in which the incipient artist himself had to handle his gradual perception of the talent that sets him apart from others.

Kerouac's account of this self-discovery takes not the conventional form of an individual's recognition of an expressive power within himself, but rather of dimly perceived figures, outside of and at first distant from himself with whom he is finally united. Doctor Sax is actually not a part of himself, a creation of his own imagination, but rather an embodiment, independent of his own body, of a capacity that he shares with other creative people and that unites them in some kind of "oversoul." (In *Book of Dreams*, he speaks of Doctor Sax as his "Lowell Dream."[7]) Much of the novel is taken up with the narrator's struggle to break away from the reassuring comfort of his family and familiar scenes in order to internalize and exploit his new power.

Just as Kerouac divides himself in *The Town and the City* between the Martin brothers, so here he portrays Ti Jean's creative development as splitting his personality. The novel, however, concentrates only on the development of one of these personalities, the "Francis Martin" voice. During the years drawn upon for this story, the "Peter Martin" side of Kerouac was also emerging on the athletic fields, but that development is ignored here for treatment later in the overlapping *Vanity of Duluoz*.

It takes a long time for young Duluoz to recognize his relationship to Doctor Sax as the story meanders through six sections that serve also to recapitulate the young Kerouac's early creative experiments. The first section, "Ghosts of the Pawtucketville Night," opens appropriately with a dream sequence, in which events from the narrator's childhood are recalled in a manner reminiscent of the early pages of Marcel Proust's *Remembrance of Things Past*. The second section, "A Gloomy Bookmovie," illustrates the kind of "home movies" that young Kerouac began creating in the early 1930s in written, then in illustrated form. Much of this section deals with the days that Duluoz, like Kerouac himself, devoted his imagination to working out an elaborate horse-racing game that the controlling artist found he could rig.

This section, which ends "God bless the children of this picture, this bookmovie,"[8] is heavily nostalgic, conveying a sense of the incipient artist's reluctance to leave both the family world into which he was born and the imaginary one that he has created for his private delight. Indeed the whole section leads up to the recognition that: "It now occurs to me my father spent most of his time when I was 13 in the winter of 1936, thinking about a hundred details to be done in the Club alone not to mention home and business shop. . . . While I sat around all the time with my little diary, my Turf, my hockey games. . . . My football games occupied me with the same seriousness of the angels—we had little time to talk to each other" (96–97).

The very brief third section, "More Ghosts," describes the young artist making another discovery that will greatly affect his fantasy life, which he describes as "something secretively wild and baleful in the glares of the child soul, the masturbatory surging triumph of the knowledge of reality" (102) that culminates in the ironic juxtaposition of his receiving the news of his pet dog's dying at exactly the climactic moment of his first autoerotic experience ("when I was lying in bed finding out that my tool had sensations in the tip" [121]).

The fourth section focuses on one of the experiences of Kerouac's own childhood that made a most profound impression upon him, "The Night the Man with the Watermelon Died," which leads to the morbid observation that "everybody in Pawtucketville had the perfect opportunity to commit suicide coming home every night—that is why we lived deep lives" (127). This section also includes the full text of what is attributed to the mysterious Doctor Sax as his only known piece of fiction, a ghoulish tale of decadent sophisticates in the forbidding "castle" that brooded over Lowell. The baroque text is exactly the kind of composition that a thirteen-year-old boy fed on fantasy fiction would consider the epitome of elegant decadence—a kind of juvenile version of Roman Polanski's *Dance of the Vampyrs* that is almost certainly either a recovery or reconstruction of one of Kerouac's earliest efforts at romancing.

The fifth section, "The Flood," returns to reality with an account of the devastating disaster that shook youthful faith in the security of life in Lowell when the Merrimack River overflowed and drowned the lowlying parts of the town. At first Duluoz and his restless young friends want the flood to "pierce thru and drown the world, the horrible adult routine world," but the narrator finally recognizes sadly that the flood has done its damage by destroying "something that can't possibly come back again in America and history, the gloom of the unaccomplished mudheap civilization when it gets caught with its pants down from a source it long lost contact with" (180).

Finally in the sixth section, "The Castle," the narrator discovers his vocation, as his vision, which has been alternating between fantasy and reality, at last moves fluidly from one to the other when a recollection of familiar nocturnal scenes in the Lowell of his childhood blend into the depiction of a struggle between superhuman forces that hold the fate of the earth in the balance. This childish, lurid fantasy, manufactured from *Weird Tales* and other pulp fantasy magazines of the 1930s, has perplexed some admirers of Kerouac's treatment of more recognizable landscapes. It also must have upset Malcolm Cowley, who suggested at one time that the novel might be published if the fantasy were cut out.[9] This culminating fantasy, however, is the indispensable reason for the existence of the book.

It must be remembered, however, that Kerouac's literary taste and style at the time this episode recalls had been fashioned by the purple prose of the pulp magazines and the "scary" radio programs of his childhood, especially "The Shadow"—an extremely popular half-hour show that celebrated the achievements of Lamont Cranston, a figure with a split personality (like the later Superman), who was a wealthy dilettante in his daylight life, but a mysterious force of good in his guise of "The Shadow." (Novelist David Madden has also recalled this nemesis of evildoers.) Kerouac is trying to create here, possibly from early writings of his own, the kind of lurid allegory that aspiring fourteen-year-olds think ponderous, a successful recapturing of the excesses of juvenilia that Joyce accomplished also in *A Portrait of the Artist as a Young Man*. To understand what led him to do this requires tracing the development of Ti Jean's relationship with Doctor Sax.

Sax is first mentioned briefly in the third paragraph of the novel: "Doctor Sax I first saw in his earlier lineaments in the early Catholic childhood of Centralville, deaths, funerals" (4), and young Duluoz senses that he is a friend, "my ghost, personal angel, private shadow, secret lover" (34). The most significant remark among these early recollections, however, is that, absorbed in the routine of Lowell life, Duluoz and his schoolboy friends, "didn't give a shit about no Doctor Sax" (40). His time has not yet come. Even this early, though, Duluoz's imagination is so hyperactive that he has to give up the church "to ease my horrors—too much candlelight, too much wax" as "Doctor Sax traversed the darknesses between pillars in the church at vespertime" (66–67).

Through the next two books Sax remains a shadowy figure with whom Ti Jean has no direct contacts; but he begins to get a sense of the peculiar power of this ghostly figure as he associates Sax with the boredom Ti Jean feels with the routine of ordinary life and the discovery of another secret source of private power in "the masturbatory surging triumph of the knowledge of reality." "Tonight Doctor Sax will stalk," the narrator proclaims, though he does not yet accompany Sax (102).

Ti Jean actually encounters Sax at last more than three-quarters of the way through the story in the final section when the narrator is standing just at nightfall one evening on a sandbank's top, surveying the familiar scenes of his childhood, "like a meditative king" (192). Suddenly he turns to see Doctor Sax standing nearby. At first Ti Jean passes out from fear of being "overcome," but he soon recovers and realizes that Sax is his friend. Together they set out on a secret investigation of the city as they peer into the homes and lives of Duluoz's longtime friends and neighbors. "Say goodbye to your view of the sand hills of where you call your home—we're going through these bushes and down to Phebe Avenue," Sax tells the boy, as "tragically" he leads him off (195).

The boy cannot yet comprehend the observations that Sax makes as they continue their eavesdropping journey, but he develops an assurance that "Doctor Sax is speaking to the bottom of my boy problems and they could all be solved if I could fathom his speech" (197). "Gliding together in the dark shadows of the night," he concludes, "Doctor Sax and I know . . . everything about Lowell" (199). "Bye and bye," Sax assures his companion, "you'll rise to the sun and propel your mean bones hard and sure to huge labors . . . but you'll never be as happy as you are now in your quiltish innocent book-devouring boyhood immortal night" (203)—both a prophecy and a warning about the road that lies ahead.

Suddenly, after Sax summarizes the peculiarly literary implications of all they have seen together with the observation that "all your America is like a dense Balzacian hive in a jewel point" (208), the scene changes. From their ghostly visit to sites in Lowell, they are transported to the ominous castle, where a titanic struggle with the Great Snake of the World will occur. Young Duluoz understandably observes, "There were things going on I couldn't fathom," although he is frightened by the prospect of Sax's confrontation with the Great

Snake. At a crucial moment, Sax's magic fails, and he is forced to meet Judgment Day not in the Shadow's cape and mask that he has been wearing, but "just poor old beatup trousers . . . a white shirt underneath, and regular brown shoes, and regular socks" (240), so that he looks something like Gary Cooper.

Sax's rueful admission at this point, "Funny thing is, I never knew that I would meet Judgment Day in my regular clothes without having to go around in the middle of the night with that silly cape" (240), seems to indicate that despite the grand guignol excesses of this last scene in the novel, Duluoz is growing away from his childhood influences and is beginning to perceive that his future as a creative writer is not going to depend on creating such Gothic claptrap, but on reconstructing scenes like those of the ordinary life in Lowell that he has just observed or of the kind of down-to-earth films in which Gary Cooper appeared (Kerouac could have had in mind a film like Frank Capra's *Mr. Deeds Goes to Town*). He is also beginning to realize, however, that he is unable—like the mythical Shadow—to control the destiny of the universe by himself when Sax is driven to the chastening reflection that "nothing works in the end, you just—there's just absolutely nothing—nobody cares what happens to you, the universe doesn't care what happens to mankind" (240–41).

This tale of the artist's discovery of his calling does not end, however, on a downbeat note, as Kerouac's later work often does. Suddenly a Bird of Paradise swoops down "to save mankind as the Snake upward protruded insinuating itself from the earth" (242), and Dr. Sax reflects with amazement, "The Universe disposes of its own evil" (245). The narrator reports that he has since seen Doctor Sax several times, "at dusk, in autumn, when the kids jump up and down and scream—he only deals in glee now" (245), but Duluoz has not entirely absorbed the creative power of Doctor Sax into his personality. He remains a divided individual, lacking a full confidence in his own creative powers and still dependent upon a last-minute rescue by a Bird of Paradise (however one may choose to interpret its significance). *Doctor Sax* remains, however, most important in understanding Kerouac's conception of the origins of his literary career. The conception of Doctor Sax is said to have been influenced by William Burroughs, whom Kerouac was visiting in Mexico at the time he was finishing the novel. Burroughs may have affected some of the specific allegories (the bird and the snake are especially prominent in ancient

Mexican mythology), but the allegorical nature of the doctor appears to have been firmly established in Kerouac's mind long before he even knew Burroughs and to have shaped itself out of the images of the Shadow and Gary Cooper, out of the radio programs and movies of the 1930s. The novel remains a remarkable tribute to the role that these figures played in liberating the talents of an artist who would produce works far different from those that inspired him.

Chapter Six

The Town and the City— *Vanity of Duluoz* and *Maggie Cassidy*

Readers must greatly readjust their perspective as they move from the mystical sentimentality of *Visions of Gerard* and the fantasies of *Doctor Sax* to the colloquial realism of *Vanity of Duluoz*, for these works were written at vastly different periods in the author's life. The first two are the work of the years before the success of *On the Road*, when Kerouac was most actively experimenting with new fictional techniques as well as dabbling in Buddhism; *Vanity of Duluoz* is the last major work that he would finish, not long before his death, the cheerless recollections of a disgruntled man, out of patience with his generation and stylistic experimentation, finished in ten exhausting bursts of writing between March and May 1967, while he was living back in Lowell. He had twice earlier started books with this title (the first while he was a sportswriter for the Lowell *Sun* in 1942), but he had abandoned both. When he finally produced the book, it was to replace the early *The Town and the City*, incorporating a fictionalization of his high school and college years into the Duluoz Legend.

Vanity of Duluoz (1935–46, 1967, 1968)

Since the two novels cover exactly the same period—from Jack Kerouac/Peter Martin/Jack Duluoz's development of a sense of identity as a football player in their thirteenth years to the deaths of their cloned fathers immediately after World War II—one is first curious to learn the extent to which the two books duplicate each other and the ways in which they differ, especially since the first was written by a vigorous, young, aspiring but unknown author while the second is the work of a tired, celebrated but disillusioned author in declining health. The answer is that there is surprisingly little duplication. The

275 pages of *Vanity of Duluoz* probably carry far fewer than half of the words of the nearly 500-page *The Town and the City* (the manuscript of which had been reduced more than half by the publishers). Most of the saving is accomplished through the omission of the adventures of the numerous Martin siblings in the earlier work that had no counterparts in reality; but, even omitting consideration of these contrived episodes, the second novel reproduces remarkably few episodes from the first, emphasizing the extremely limited extent to which *The Town and the City* can be called autobiographical and made compatible with the Duluoz Legend. The tone of the works is also vastly different; Kerouac felt in 1967 that there was "no time for poetry,"[1] and *Vanity of Duluoz* is permeated by a world weariness in marked contrast to the ecstatic concept of the romantic mysteriousness of life that flavors the earlier novel, written under Thomas Wolfe's influence.

Comparison of the treatment in the two novels of the events that are drawn from Kerouac's own life sheds light, however, not only on actual happenings of the years that provided "An Adventurous Education," as he subtitles *Vanity of Duluoz*, but also on which of these made the most lasting impressions upon him and the way that he had come to recall them after two decades during which he had moved from obscurity to celebrity into a self-imposed withdrawal from the principal scenes of this education.

Both novels begin with accounts of an adolescent's success on the football field based on Kerouac's own experiences in Lowell. The later book, however, contains far more specific information about those games that Kerouac recalls in detail, but it does not linger, as the earlier one did, on the winning touchdown in the final high school game that made Kerouac's local reputation and attracted national attention to him. A comparison of the handling of this first climactic moment in both novels well illustrates the difference between their styles and tones:

And now suddenly the crowd rose to its feet with one roaring cry of surprise, explosive and vast, as a Galloway player swept wide around the end, leaped into the air, twisted, and shot the ball several yards over dark helmeted heads, as another Galloway player paused, twisted, reached out for the ball, barely grasped it in his fingers, turned and went plummeting downfield along the sidelines . . . [another hundred words of excited description omitted] finally diving over and rolling in the end zone triumphantly. (*The Town and the City*, 79–80) a few plays later Kelakis flips me a 3-yard lob over the outside end's hands and I take this ball and turn down the sidelines and bash and drive head down, head up, pause, move on. Downing throws a beautiful block, somebody else too, bumping I go, 18 yards, and just make it to the goal line where a Lawrence guy hits me and hangs on but I just jump out of his arms and over on my face with the game's only touchdown. (*Vanity of Duluoz*, 23)

Kerouac's further football career also figures largely in the action of four out of the thirteen books into which *Vanity of Duluoz* is divided. These include a bitter account, not paralleled in *The Town and the City*, of the pressure that rival college football coaches place on Kerouac's family. Whereas Peter Martin in *The Town and the City* attended a prep school in Maine and then went to the University of Pennsylvania, Duluoz follows Kerouac's exact path to a prep school in New York City and then to Columbia University. Like Peter, Jack Duluoz (Kerouac uses in the later novel his own nickname) also quits the football team during his sophomore year; but, unlike Peter, who never returns to college, Duluoz comes back once again, as Kerouac did, to make a second and most dramatic break. The portrayal of the two moments of decision differ greatly; the second is much less florid and more specific:

And gazing out the window at the campus [Peter Martin] suddenly felt a great loathing rise in him. "And now I'm supposed to go to football practice!" he cried out in the room and, jumping up, he pulled the shade down and plunged the room in dreary half darkness. He sat down again at the desk, peering in the gloom at his father's letter. . . . "It's human life I want—the thing itself—not this," he said to himself with happy surprise. . . .
He had decided to quit the football team, he was not going to play any more football. (*The Town and the City*, 262–63)

"*Now* coach?" I'm saying to Lu at the bench on the Army game on Saturday and he doesn't even look my way.
So the following Monday, snow in my window and Beethoven on the radio, Fifth Symphony, I say to myself, "Okay, I quit football." (*Vanity of Duluoz*, 151)

Kerouac's first serious romance with Mary Carney in Lowell had been assigned in *The Town and the City* not to football player Peter, but his sophisticated intellectual sibling Francis. In *Vanity of Duluoz*, since the narrator is "not talking about my women, or ex-women, in this book because it's about football and war" (198), the affair is acknowledged by football-playing Duluoz, but only in passing, with the advice to interested readers that this "first love affair with Maggie Cassidy" has been "recorded in novel of same name in detail."[2] The only substantial account of any of Duluoz's relationships with a woman in *Vanity* is the description of the events leading up to an emergency marriage that parallels Kerouac's to Edie Parker (here called Johnnie)—an event that is not chronicled in *The Town and the City*.

Both novels describe the protagonist's experience during his first voyage with the merchant marine, though in *The Town and the City*, the *Dorchester* is called the *Westminister*, and there is no account of a drunken unauthorized leave in Nova Scotia. Both novels include elaborate accounts of a psychiatric discharge from the navy, like the one that Kerouac himself received, although in the early novel this is part of brother Francis's history. (Peter Martin's way of handling his military obligation is never clarified.) Francis begins his campaign by feigning continual headaches, not by "suddenly [laying] my gun down into the dust and just walk[ing] away from everybody forever more" during a military drill, as Kerouac himself did and describes Duluoz as doing in *Vanity* (156).

Both novels devote substantial space to another ugly matter, the Lucien Carr/David Kammerer affair that ended with Carr's killing of his pursuer. In *The Town and the City*, however, Kammerer (here called Waldo Meister) commits suicide, so that neither Peter Martin nor his friend are ever arrested and jailed, and there is no indication that Meister's pursual of Kenny Wood has a homosexual motive, as Kammerer's did. In *Vanity of Duluoz*, this whitewashed account of an event that deeply affected Kerouac is replaced by what is apparently as an exact a record of the actual course of events as Kerouac could recall. The point of including the episode in *The Town and the City* was to provide an indication of mother and father Martin's horror at their discovery of the dreadful company son Peter was keeping; in *Vanity of Duluoz* the emphasis shifts to Jack's horror at his involvement with murder and the frightening conditions that he encounters in jail.

Both novels end with the death of the protagonist's father under circumstances paralleling the death of Leo Kerouac from stomach cancer; but whereas in *The Town and the City* the description of the burial in New Hampshire extends over eighteen sentiment-drenched pages, in *Vanity of Duluoz* the narrator comments only: "So the undertakers come and dump him in a basket and we have him hearsed up to the cemetery in New Hampshire in the town where he was born and little idiot birds are singing on the branch" (278).

The first novel was an attempt to transform some events from Kerouac's life and even more from a rich adolescent imagination into an appealing tale for readers, especially the many who then admired the works of Thomas Wolfe; it was the work of an ambitious and still quite naive young person trying to find a remunerative career doing what he most wished to do. The second is an account, written as the author's explanation of an important part of his past to his wife, in which a tired and disillusioned celebrity attempts to set the record straight for her—and through her the world—and to recapture a dwindling audience for his works.

Considered strictly on its own merits, *Vanity of Duluoz* shows considerable technical improvement over Kerouac's apprentice work. Even this late in his career he was carefully calculating devices that would give his work greater structural unity. While his addressing the narrative to "wifey dear" may grate feminist sensibilities (for which Kerouac never showed any particular concern), his intentions seem to have been maudlin rather than condescending, and he does not overwork the device. The terseness of the style and the concentration on a few major incidents, told with particular attention to specific names, times, and places, makes this last work much more graphic than many of the earlier ones, so that one regrets that Kerouac was never able to go back and reshape the whole Legend.

What particularly distinguishes *Vanity of Duluoz* from earlier works—to the distress often of fans of those works—are the running comments that support those in essays he wrote during the 1960s providing evidence of his state of mind, especially when he sought to go home again to Lowell. Explaining the title of this new novel, the former prophet of the Beat Generation avows, "No 'generation' is 'new.' There's 'nothing new under the sun.' 'All is vanity!' " (279), harking back to the language of *Ecclesiastes* also echoed in Ernest Hemingway's world-weary chronicle of an earlier "lost generation" in *The Sun Also Rises*.

Kerouac's final "particular form of anguish," we learn from the paragraph-long sentence that opens the novel, "came from being too sensitive to all the lunkheads I had to deal with just so I could get to be a high school football star . . . and God help me, a WRITER, whose very 'success!' far from being a happy triumph as of old, was the sign of doom Himself" (7). Not all the blame, however, he acknowledges, could be placed on the lunkheads, for he also confides, "I had goofed throughout entire wartime and this is my confession" (272).

But lunkheads do abound, as Kerouac had been taught to believe. Something of the atmosphere in which Duluoz grew up is suggested by Papa Emil's tirade when he comes to see why his son is being held in a naval hospital: "Good boy! tell that goddamn Roosevelt and his ugly wife where to get off! All a bunch of Communists. The Germans should not be our enemies but our Allies. This is a war for the Marxist Communist Jews and you are a victim of the whole plot" (163). That Duluoz himself has developed similar sentiments and learned the error of his innocent boyhood ways becomes apparent from one of the few specifically political statements in his work, as he is reminiscing about the days before World War II when "we were all pro-Lenin, or pro-whatever Communists, it was before we found out that Henry Fonda in *Blockade* [a 1938 film about the Spanish Civil War] was not such a great anti-Fascist idealist at all, just the reverse of the coin of Fascism, *i.e.*, what the hell's the difference between Fascist Hitler and anti-Fascist Stalin, or, as today, Fascist Lincoln Rockwell and anti-Fascist Ernesto Guevara, or name your own?" (85). He goes on to question Columbia College for having him study the writings of Communist ideologists when "all the time the architect is that invisible monster known as Living Man?" This "monster" he finds responsible for the appalling state of affairs that compels him to ask in 1967: "what possible feeling can be left in me for an 'America' that has become such a potboiler of broken convictions, messes of rioting and fighting in streets, hoodlumism, cynical administration of cities and states, suits and neckties the only feasible subject, grandeur all gone into the mosaic mesh of Television" (106).

"Eviscerated of 1930's innocent ambition," he observes, "everybody looks at everybody else on the sidewalk with guilt and worse than that, curiosity and faked concern" (15, 8). The road that Peter Martin had taken at the end of *The Town and the City*, Jack Duluoz finally has found has led nowhere. For those already familiar with Kerouac *Vanity of Duluoz* is a fascinating, if sad account of what became of a person who might have become a shaper of a new era; but the novel introduces into Kerouac's self-legend only the point already made in *On the Road* that one's energies run out, expanded to the gen-eralization that everyone's energies do. Thus the Duluoz Legend pre-sents finally a defeatist vision.

Maggie Cassidy (1938–39, 1953, 1959)

The story of Kerouac/Duluoz's education cannot, however, be con-cluded without harking back from this disillusioned vision of 1967 to an earlier picture of an earlier time, the account of a first romance that needs to be inserted into the recital earlier in this chapter of the events of the transitional years during which the young adventurer moved from the town to the city.

Most heroic quests, even the great Gatsby's, have been inspired by the desire to win the hand and heart of a beautiful woman. Whatever Kerouac's romantic orientation, however, women seem only to have played a destructive role in it. One of the most frustrating problems to be considered in contemplating the Duluoz Legend, in fact, is that if the hero was in pursuit of some grail, determining what it might have been. Certainly it was never a fair maiden.

"From sweet Lowell Maggie came to sour New York in a rosy gown,"[3] Duluoz chants at the critical transitional point in *Maggie Cassidy*. Almost all the drama of this downbeat romance is packed into its final fifteen pages. The first ninety percent of the short work is a lyrical preparation for the narrator's rite of passage that will sweep him into a new society into which he will not be able to carry a bride—even if he wishes to.

Writing by hand in Brooklyn during the winter months of early 1953 during the most productive period of his career, Kerouac was at the height of his literary power when, following *Doctor Sax*, he turned to the next episode in his early history, his sensibility still dominated by the voice of Francis Martin. Rarely has anyone captured so well the hysterical disappointments of infatuation mistaken for love (in *The Town and the City*, Kerouac had attributed the whole affair to the volatile Francis rather than the stolid Peter). "If you want to marry me ever don't ever try to have me come to this New York," Maggie screams at one point, "The hell with all these people" (182). "They're my friends," Duluoz replies coolly. "Maggie lost," he ex-plains, articulating the reasons for the choice that has been thrust upon him. She returns to Lowell, while he remains in New York "on the lyrical perfect shelf of America in the night, the Apple on the Rock" (188).

The long buildup to this brief conclusion may seem overly digressive, but Kerouac is not simply chronicling the highlights of a doomed romance. Because Maggie becomes the only thread that might hold him to his childhood environment, he is using the account of their affair to create a panoramic picture of his whole relationship to Lowell, Massachusetts, at the end of the innocent 1930s.

The first four sections of the book are narrated in the third person, describing in minute detail the conversation and relationships of six teenaged boys, five French-Canadians and one of Greek extraction, as they are walking through the snow to a New Year's Eve dance. In the fifth section, the narration changes to first person; the action zooms in on Jack Duluoz when the boys arrive at the Rex Ballroom and the others fade into the crowd as Jack is introduced to Maggie Cassidy. The at first inconspicuous shift in the narrative mode is impeccably appropriate to the telling of this story. Something is happening at this dawning of 1939; sixteen-year-old Jack Duluoz is entering a new phase of his experience, so that even what has happened only a few minutes previously, the product of relationships built up through many years of childhood, must be looked back upon by a different person, who has separated himself from the group and who sees the "me" of then as the "him" of now. The "I" of the narrative springs into being at the moment of the meeting with Mary.

Through most of the novel, the account of the hesitantly developing romance is sandwiched between recollections of other experiences that Jack will treasure from the Lowell past, especially his prowess as a high school track star. Some friction is generated by a rival girl friend, reluctant to give up Jack, but he has never taken her seriously and even demonstrates what their first kiss was like with one of his male buddies.

As the reader soon surmises, however, the romance with Mary is only infatuation; even at this time Jack is something of an old-fashioned boy who is never able or willing to consummate his relationship with Maggie. He finally confesses that he had had his "first sex with a red-headed older girl a professional whore" in midtown New York (176). When on the New Year's anniversary of their first meeting Maggie wants him to do with her what he did to "them girls in New York," he recoils; "Aw Maggie I can't do that to you" (177). He thinks it too "sinful bigcity." Without using the term he is casting himself in the role of a courtly lover. His behavior would suit a quest myth, but the times are wrong for such chivalry.

He is too knightly, however, to accuse her of what has also become obvious to the reader—that as a high school dropout (as we learn from her rival for Jack's attentions), Maggie is desperately anxious to get married and settle down in order to secure her precarious position in Lowell. She has no aspirations to move beyond there. She begins to press her attentions upon him; but, although he observes that "we practically did everything there is to do," he never "touched her in the prime focal points. . . . We didn't know where we were, what to do" (74). She knows where they are, though, for she tells him, "I want to go home to a house to sleep with you and be married." "I drooped to think about it," he writes, "I had no idea what I should do" (146). When she tries to play him off against a rival, he finds that he is growing more fond of her, but he still pouts "like a big baby over the thought of losing my home and going off into the unknown suicides of weddings and honeymoons" (150). (The ominous word *suicide* shows what a different view of marriage his is from hers, and it may provide a clue to the continuing state of Kerouac's mind.)

As he finds it difficult to make dates with her, he goes off to prep school in New York without making any kind of arrangements with her about the future. Settled at his mother's stepmother's in Brooklyn, he begins to expand his dreams: "My dream has in it a wife beautiful beyond belief, not Maggie, some gorgeous new blonde gold sexpot of starry perfection. . . . I pictured the gorgeous Gene Tierney" (167). When Maggie at last writes that she is "terribly sorry" about all that she has done, Jack invites her to the prom at the prep school. Here she is snubbed by his friends' fashionable New York dates, and after her outburst about never wanting to come to New York, Jack finds "the two of us miles apart in social fear" (180).

Jack sums up the outcome of the ill-starred weekend: "[The girls] went back home on Monday morning after a night's sleep, Maggie to her porch, her kid sisters, her swains coming a-visiting down the road, her river, her night—I to my whirlpools of new litter and glitter" (187). A chilling epilogue presents the more mature Duluoz's response to his recollections of the affair.

Three years later, just about to enter the navy, he returns to Lowell and makes a date with Maggie. When he attempts to seduce her in the back seat of a Buick at two o'clock in the morning, he finds "the sweetness of the girl was hidden from the boy by a thick rubber girdle at which he pulled and yanked, desperately drunk, poised at the gate" (194). She laughs in his face before he drives her back home and, we gather, out of his life forever. "Just a little hometown scene on a Saturday night," as Jack commented much earlier about a more innocent experience that sums up the "sweetness" of the so often depressing 1930s. *Maggie Cassidy* is a charming ironic tale about the struggle that many young Americans have faced between the demands of the town and the city, but both characters lack the dimensions of legendary figures. The tale does not have the power of the confrontation scene in the Plaza Hotel in *The Great Gatsby*, because both characters sell out too quickly and too cheaply. As Francis Martin, despite his lofty literary talk, Kerouac is closer to Ring Lardner than to Scott Fitzgerald. Read together, *Vanity of Duluoz* and *Maggie Cassidy* present a consistent picture, despite differences between them, of a young man who knows that he wants to get out of town but does not know where he wants to go.

Chapter Seven
On the Road—
Visions of Cody

We have already observed in chapter 3 that Kerouac's most familiar and popular work, *On the Road*, does not really fit into the final form of the Duluoz Legend as Kerouac left it, because, it was superseded by a greatly expanded account of the early relationship between the characters based on Kerouac himself and Neal Cassady (Sal Paradise and Dean Moriarity in *On the Road*; Jack Duluoz and Cody Pomeray in *Visions of Cody* and the other authentic parts of the Legend). *Visions of Cody*, as Kerouac finally titled his personal favorite among his works, was not, however, only the second version that Kerouac projected of the same basic work. Although Tim Hunt was denied access to the manuscripts that might conclusively resolve many problems, he has argued convincingly, on the basis of letters, journals and the texts themselves, that it was, in fact, the fifth.[1]

For the detailed evidence in support of these claims, anyone seriously interested in Kerouac's literary achievement must consult Hunt's *Kerouac's Crooked Road*, the best critical study so far published of this often underrated artist. It is sufficient here to outline the argument developed from Hunt's detective work in order to suggest the place of Kerouac's most ambitious undertaking—published in its entirety only after his death—in the overall Duluoz Legend.

According to Hunt's reconstruction, the process of shaping the "road" novel began in the fall of 1948, immediately following Kerouac's completion of *The Town and the City*. The new novel was planned as a follow-up to the previous one, picking up where it left off and describing in much the same style the adventures of a character named Ray Smith—a name that Kerouac used again years later for his alter ego in *The Dharma Bums*. (It is not clear why Kerouac dropped the concept of the Martin family after the first novel, but he was growing away from Wolfe's influence and was probably beginning to find the large tribe unwieldy.) The new novel was to be writ-

ten in the third person, and, as Kerouac progressed in his work on
it, he became increasingly intrigued with the use of a kind of Dreiser-
esque "factualism" in the narrative.[2] Hunt thinks, however, that Kerouac wrote no more than thirty thousand words of this never
published version and that he had stopped work on it before Christmas 1948.[3]

By March 1949, he was at work on another version of the same
material, but this time the central figure was named Red Moultrie.
He was a man somewhat like Neal Cassady, whose "background, log-
ically, does not explain his spiritual nature."[4] Kerouac apparently did
little work on this version, however, and by November he was explaining still another version to an admirer named Ellen Lucey, whom
he told that his second book was already one-third completed. He described it as being about the little black boy from North Carolina,
who finally broke into print as Pic in the last work Kerouac completed during his lifetime. Hunt could not establish conclusively
whether that book is largely the earlier unfinished one or a fresh start
made late in life, though, as discussed in chapter 4, the latter possibility seems unlikely.

We do know that by April 1951 Kerouac had changed his mind
sufficiently to type on a single roll of paper what he called "the 20-
day On the Road," the basic text for the version published in 1957.
He began thinking about still further changes, however, only a few
days later, and by July he wrote Allen Ginsberg that he had decided
to cut the work and insert new passages.[5] Kerouac's discovery of
"sketching," which he later called "spontaneous prose," in October
1951 resulted in what is now the published version of On the Road
being superseded by what finally came to be called Visions of Cody. In
just about a year, Kerouac had completely refashioned the novel, using a drastically different style to achieve a new aim. Citing a letter
from Kerouac to Ginsberg on 18 May 1952, Hunt pinpoints the difference between the two works: "On the Road ceased to be a traditional
survey of travelling and became instead a project that consciously and
unconsciously evoked Cassady in his many dimensions."[6]

Ginsberg was skeptical at first about the transformation. He wrote
Cassady that the new version was "a log of meaningless bullshit I
think, page after page of surrealist free association that don't make
sense to anybody except someone who has blown Jack."[7] He proved
correct in his further assumption that no one would publish it. After
the success of On the Road, James Laughlin's New Directions did pub-

lish some excerpts in a limited edition in 1959, but the whole text did not become available until 1972, several years after Kerouac's death. By that time, Ginsberg had changed his mind and offered in an introduction called "The Great Rememberer," a useful breakdown of the six-part structure of the work, which he hailed as "a work of primitive genius," comparable to Henri Rousseau's paintings.

The first two of these six parts are simply numbered. The third is both numbered and titled "Frisco: The Tape." The fourth and fifth parts are titled "Imitation of the Tape" and "Joan Rawshanks in the Fog," respectively, while the sixth simply begins after a break in the text with neither a number nor a title. Ginsberg explains that the first two parts are "candid observation of inner consciousness manifested in solitude"; whereas "the entire tape section's a set of nights on newly discovered Grass, wherein these souls explored the mind blank impressions that tea creates" (both "grass" and "tea" were 1950s slang terms for marijuana). He is still not really happy with the obscurities of the fourth and fifth sections, but he speaks of them enthusiastically as "inspired rhythmic babble."

There is actually a considerably more careful structure to the work than this gloss suggests; the book is closer to a conventional novel pattern than has usually been recognized, although the style and odd points of view distract the reader from the underlying plan.

The tale is triggered by the narrator's desire to see once again Cody Pomeray, Duluoz's great buddy from his days on the road. The very first sentence is heavy with nostalgia: "This is an old diner like the ones Cody and his father ate in."[8] He employs his newly discovered technique of "sketching" to set the scene, as he begins the third of twenty-nine sections making up the first part of the book, "In the autumn of 1951 I began thinking of Cody Pomeray" (5). Through the next forty pages he sketches the places he visits and the things that bring Cody to mind (including the narrator's masturbating in the men's room of an old Third Avenue El station on New York's East Side). Gradually, as experience piles on experience and memory on memory, he works up the enthusiasm to write an excited letter to Cody informing him of "my trip to Frisco at last to stay with you and talk with you and really be with it 100% for any number of inexpressibly delicious weeks you wish" (38).

The second section (47–116) consists of another twenty-six sketches. The first eleven of these are considerably longer than most others in the first two sections of the novel. They are also done in traditionally narrative style rather than impressionistically, describing what Duluoz is able to reconstruct from secondhand knowledge of Cody's life before they met, beginning with Cody's acceptance at the age of fifteen into Denver poolhall society when he met Tom Watson on a Saturday afternoon in October 1942. The action switches, however, about two-thirds of the way through this second section to a detailed description of Duluoz's cross-country trip after he fails to get an expected berth on a merchant marine ship bound for San Francisco. The twenty-second section is a fast, fragmented account of the principal events of this journey.

The third—and by far the longest—section of the novel (117–246)—begins without any introductory explanation a transcription of either the whole texts or a series of excerpts from five tapes recorded over five nights at Cassady's home by Kerouac and Cassady (here, of course, identified as Jack and Cody), with Cassady's wife, Carolyn (here called Evelyn), sometimes joining in, and with three others identified only as Pat, Jimmy, and Ed participating occasionally. From the recorded conversations, we learn that the tapes were made between the time that the participants had begun smoking marijuana in order to get high and the time that either the conversation had become incomprehensible or the tape had run out unnoticed. While many things (some of which mean nothing to the reader) are discussed, the principal purpose of the conversations appears to have been Jack's efforts to coax out of Cody complete accounts of some events at which Jack was not present. These are generally unsuccessful because Cody maneuvers to avoid being pinned down too specifically. The last tape ends with a fragment from a radio broadcast of a revival meeting at a black church.

The fourth section of the book, "Imitation of the Tape" (249–74), is the most obscure section of the narrative. Using a stream-of-consciousness style similar to that of James Joyce's *Ulysses*, Kerouac is evidently attempting to find a way to create imaginatively the spontaneousness of the taped dialogues. At its most ambitious, this effort takes the form of a fifteen-page section (275–92), in which, as Tim Hunt convincingly explains, Duluoz becomes "scriptwriter, director, technician, bit player, star, audience, and critic," with "his awareness of the process of film as a metaphor for writing provid[ing] the key for structuring performances into a single text."[9] (Ginsberg made no attempt in his introduction to account for this passage.)

Without any major break being indicated, the Joan Rawshanks

fantasy breaks off and the narrator returns in a new paragraph beginning, "But you can't say that anything really tremendous happened to Cody and me till the summer of 1949 when I went out West to find him" (292). This leads into the account of the several "Visions of Cody" that Duluoz has had (295–307), which give the book its title and thus seem to be intended as the high point of the narrative. After this we return to a section that includes material in the form of the earlier transcription from the tapes, although it is not clear whether these conversations are actually transcriptions or "imitations" of the tapes (307–37).

The two great visions of Cody that Jack records are far too long to quote and impossible to summarize. One occurred in 1948, two years after he had first met Cody, and the second in Mexico at some unspecified time, but probably during the disastrous trip in 1950. The great point of the visions, however, appears to have been that on the second occasion, Jack saw "with eyes of fire or on fire . . . everything not only about [Cody] but America, all of America as it has become conceptualized in my brain" (297). Duluoz's ultimate vision thus appears to have been that Cody/Neal was not so important in himself as he was as the embodiment of Duluoz/Kerouac's reaction to his country and culture; and this reaction appears to be summed up in the following comment about Cody (and hence America) as "my greatest enemy—because while I saw him as an angel, a god, etcetera, I also saw him as a devil, an old witch, even an old bitch from the start" (298). Thus the revelation toward which "the Neal book" had been moving through all the false starts, was the narrator's perhaps only momentary perception of his own split personality. What would have been seen as "angel and god" by the alienated intellectual Francis Martin and the Beat congeries, would have been perceived as "devil and witch" by the piously traditionalist Peter Martin counseled by his mother modeled on Gabrielle Kerouac. *Visions of Cody* may have been Kerouac's own favorite, not just because of the stylistic achievement, which was only his means to an end, but because for once—and perhaps the only time—he had achieved a perfect equilibrium in his vision, which allowed him to see the figure that he had made into the symbol of an entire culture from two diametrically opposed viewpoints at the same time.

It is likely that the achievement of this equilibrium is responsible for the differences in point of view informing what was published as *On the Road* and the final section of *Visions of Cody* (338–98), which is a straightforward but much condensed account of the same experiences as provided the basis for the 1957 novel. As Hunt explains in detail, the effect of the two works is markedly different: "In *On the Road*, Sal laments his loss of Dean and Dean's falling away from his earlier heroic stature. In *Visions of Cody*, Duluoz's lament is also a celebration."[10] The final version of the "Neal book" ends on a surprisingly upbeat note in contrast to the downbeat conclusion of the more famous predecessor.

Since the sixty-page section is only about one-fifth the length of *On the Road*, much from that book has been omitted or condensed, especially nearly everything dealing with relationships with women, including the idyllic account of Sal's brief romance with Terry the Mexican girl. Gone also is the structure that gives the familiar novel much of its power through the repetition of the inflation-deflation pattern of the individual sections and the work as a whole. The final section of *Visions of Cody* follows more the pattern of a unified confession than of an episodic picaresque tale.

The advantage of this compression is that the later version makes more explicit feelings and points of view that are only latent in *On the Road* (and that Kerouac probably only discovered during the rewriting). Curiously in a work that has been, through most of its length, essentially *presentational* (that is, like much modern painting, it seeks not to represent events but to present the audience with a construct for its own interpretation), the final section deals more with Duluoz's reactions to the matters he discusses than with sketching the events themselves (as Hunt maintains, Sal Paradise "tells his story," while Duluoz "meditates on his story"[11]. Thus this section functions in much the same way as the final section of William Faulkner's *The Sound and the Fury*, providing us with guideposts to interpret the three previous stream-of-consciousness sections.

Duluoz explains the events on the road only enough to try to define the feelings for Cody that have motivated his quest. "I thought Cody was, and still do, one of the most remarkable men I've ever seen," he comments, adding that "the thing I couldn't get over then was the magnificence of the actual car trip" (346–48), a comment echoing Faust's on one of Mephistopheles's marvels. As in *On the Road*, however, the relationship begins to deteriorate; Duluoz confides that "everything blew out on that Cadillac trip East, there's nothing left" (374). Once again the final break occurs in Mexico City, which Duluoz describes bluntly as "the bottom of and the end of the road"

(384), where he realizes that "Cody doesn't realize how much I love him" (389). (Much of the needling conversation recorded on the tapes introduced earlier can be seen as an effort to get at the reasons for Cody's deficiency.)

The greatest change between the two accounts, however, is in their endings. In place of the dejected defeatism about the coming of night and old age at the end of *On the Road*, *Visions of Cody* ends not in Peter Martin's broken-down East but in the beckoning West with "a new day . . . dawning in the blue lagoon east over Oakland there." Although Duluoz admits, "I am made of loss," he adds, "I am made of Cody, too," but now "Cody is blank at last," and he is prepared to say, "Adios, King" to the man who had watched the sun go down with him. Now Duluoz watches the sun rise "across the fences of Golden Southern America in her Dawn" (397–98).

In the months immediately following the completion of the work published as *On the Road*, Kerouac had undergone a change of mind that freed him from the hold Cassady had had upon him, so that he could contemplate resuming their relationship, but in a manner that would give him a greater control over it than he had previously exercised. Looking at this change with respect to the Peter/Francis split that we have been observing in Kerouac's personality as it is reflected in his writings, we may theorize that in an exhausted state at the end of the marathon composition of the *On the Road* scroll, "Francis" had temporarily succumbed to "Peter." Upon reflection, though, the Francis voice was still strong enough to reassert itself and to impel Kerouac into undertaking what was to be his most complex, ambitious, and best balanced work.

Indeed the final pages of *Visions of Cody* contain the most remarkable conscious acknowledgment anywhere in Kerouac's work of the far-reaching split within himself. Meditating on the ambiguous relationship to Cody that he has recognized in his Mexican "vision," Duluoz observes, "let's hear what my French-Canadian side has to say about him" (362). There follows a page, actually split down the middle, with a Quebecois text on the left and an English version on the right, the gist of which is the advice to let Cody go—"he is your friend, let him dream; he's not your brother, he's not your father, he's not your Saint Michael. . . . Go find your soul. . . . Go find God in the nights" (362). Since French-Canadian was the language of Kerouac's childhood and English an exotic tongue learned through education and reading, the voice speaking in the language of childhood would be the hometown traditionalist addressing the rebellious "Francis," who had dominated Kerouac's vision since the publication of *The Town and the City*. The public's quick loss of interest in that book had evidently strongly shaken "Peter's" hold on Kerouac's imagination.

The more optimistic ending of *Visions of Cody* would be a primary reason, even without considering the author's preferences, for insisting that it replace *On the Road* in the Duluoz Legend, since it reveals most firmly Kerouac's psychical condition after his most comprehensive contemplation of the materials. The two novels could not both be accommodated into a collective framework, although the more famous book still merits its autonomous position as an American classic that does not so much reveal the sensibility of the Beat Generation as of a recurrent romantic type in the human personality. Sal Paradise's final soliloquy in *On the Road* recalls the nostalgia of James Fenimore Cooper's Leatherstocking, but Jack Duluoz's at the end of *Visions of Cody* echoes Walt Whitman.

Thus anyone interested in developing a comprehensive perspective on the vision revealed through Kerouac's work must cope with *Visions of Cody*, despite some formidable difficulties that it presents. Even Hunt in his sympathetic analysis of the work is obliged to admit that "the sketching of the first section tends to veer toward the private and purely imaginative world of dream," observing that "if at times the first two sections of *Visions of Cody* seem almost too dense, the tapes seem slack."[12] Apparently working in an expansive and ebullient mood during this final composition, Kerouac gave free rein to narcissistic self-indulgence; a reader must put up with a good deal while struggling through the first three-hundred pages in order to gain the rewards of the last one hundred.

The abridged version that appeared in 1959 is indeed a great deal more readable than the complete version, yet it so entirely misrepresents Kerouac's intentions that it is worthless.[13] While the novel may constitute a stumbling-block to comprehending the Duluoz Legend, it deserves the same respect as any author's experiments to break through to a new mode of expression. It is important indeed to the Legend that Kerouac tried to create that he never attempted another work of this magnitude or experimented with devices like the tape transcriptions again. Both in its form and in the narrator's concluding posture, it is the high point of the Legend and of the author's career.

Hunt, in fact speculates whether "if *Visions of Cody* had been published before *On the Road* and followed by the book that Kerouac wrote next, *Doctor Sax*, rather [than] by the much later and much shallower *Dharma Bums*, Kerouac might not have been regarded much more seriously than he has been."[14]

Quite probably he would have, but such speculations only start us down yet another crooked road; for if Kerouac had come to be recognized as an important experimenter, like Burroughs, what then? Would small success have been enough to encourage him to continue to develop a small cult following, rather than the large audience that *On the Road* attracted? Conceivably he could have survived more successfully than he did as a kind of prophet-guru instead of being destroyed as he was by privacy-invading Beatniks, but he was never equipped to handle the public in the way that Allen Ginsberg has. And suppose, after all, *On the Road* had also appeared in its turn? Would its reception and his position have been any different? Might he not finally have ended up, whatever the turnings of the road, as the presiding spirit of something like the Naropa Institute for Disembodied Poetics? For this is just what his fate has been.

After *Visions of Cody*, his only really considerable attempt at experimental writing was *Old Angel Midnight*, in which the Angel orders him, "let's hear the Sound of the Universe, son, & no more part twaddle."[15] He seems to have undertaken this project, which was probably too much influenced by Joyce, with considerable relish when he was visiting Gary Snyder in California in 1956, but his confidence in it soon petered out, and the full text has only recently been collected. The slender work adds, so far as it can be decrypted, little to the Duluoz Legend, except the very fact that he did undertake such a work in the tradition of Joyce and Gertrude Stein without any of their serious theoretical programs in mind. The sounds of the universe eluded him.

Chapter Eight

Passings Through—
Tristessa, Desolation Angels,
Book of Dreams

One of the problems about the Duluoz Legend as the kind of comprehensive saga that Kerouac envisioned is that after his years on road with Neal Cassady, he was not able to find in his life elements of conflict powerful enough to provide the substance for works with the narrative coherence and direction of *Visions of Gerard*, *Doctor Sax*, *Maggie Cassidy*, and the "Neal Book" as it took final shape in *Visions of Cody*. All of these were really meditations on losses—the loss of a beloved brother in childhood, loss of childhood innocence (though more than compensated for in *Doctor Sax* by the gaining of creative power), loss of romantic idealism and sexual innocence in *Maggie Cassidy*, and the failure of friendship to provide a stable, unifying element in his life. Nothing after Duluoz's reconciliation with the realities of Cody's inadequacies involved him passionately enough to provide an adequate dramatic vehicle for shaping fragments of his experience into fiction with a seeming universal significance. After the failure of *The Town and the City* to establish his reputation, he had really for the moment nothing more to lose. Although his breakdown was a long time coming, Kerouac's personality had begun to disintegrate by 1952 in that often foreboding "thirtieth year" of a poet's life.

He produced no works that by any extension of the term can be called "novels" based on events between 1952 and 1959 (and actually there will only be one true novel about subsequent events to serve as capstone to the Legend). He was principally busy, of course, from 1952 to 1956, the most productive period of his life, giving shape to the legend of his early years, and—unlike some of his contemporaries—he was not intrigued by the idea of writing novels about writing novels. He also surely never planned to attempt to write about what he calls in *Desolation Angels*, "the horror of my literary notoriety,"[1] although fragments of material about his experiences during these years provide the bases for a variety of works in several manners. None of these, however, is experimental in the sense that *Visions of Cody* had been. His life has often seemed more interesting than his fiction because he never dealt adequately in the fiction with those years when he was most in the public eye. Before moving on to the climax of the Legend, we must look, however, at the ways in which Kerouac assembled bits and pieces from experiences in places that he "passed through" (borrowing the title of the second part of *Desolation Angels*) during what were to prove in retrospect the Beat years.

Tristessa (1955–56, 1960)

Although published separately as a novel, *Tristessa* is hardly more than a two-part short story about an impressionable American visitor's encounter in the slums of Mexico City with a tragically beautiful dope addict and other exotic types.[2] While the tale is linked to the Duluoz Legend, it is essentially a genre piece, a harking back to such eighteenth-century sentimental romances as Goethe's *Sorrows of Young Werther* or the Abbe Prevost's *Manon Lescaut.* Kerouac's most stylized work, its picture of the two-dimensional narrator who is largely limited to an observer's role does not jibe with the portrayal of the complex character summoned up in the other volumes of the Legend.

Most of the limited criticism of this book, which was long out of print, concentrates on nourishing the notion that Kerouac's life was indeed more interesting than his work by ferreting out the details of the real-life events on which the story is based or on taking seriously the narrator's Werther-like posturings ("I moan to recover all that magic, remembering my own *impending* death."[3]) The stereotype of the bug-eyed tourist discovering how the other half lives is too strongly suggested by lines like, "I watch truly amazed, stoned as I am, I can see this must be the biggest junk den in Latin America— what interesting types! (78). He also has a duffelbag full of notions about the joys of the underprivileged: "Everything is so poor in Mexico . . . and yet everything they do is happy and carefree" (29). (Some material like this also surfaces in *Visions of Cody.*)

Previous commentators seem not to have lingered long enough over the concluding lines of the book, "I'll write long sad tales about people in the legend of my life—This part is my part of the movie, let's hear yours" (96). Though not very long, *Tristessa* is long enough to make its point, and it is surely almost unrelievedly sad (the name of the heroine—if the term is appropriate—means "sad little woman"). Not much actually happens in the story. Tristessa is in bad shape when the narrator meets her, and she steadily deteriorates. When he returns to Mexico a year after their first encounter to check up on her, he is told by an American who has settled permanently south of the border to provide a home for his morphine addiction, "I don't know what's the matter with her, she's changed in the past two weeks, the *past week* even—" (64). By the end of the story she has collapsed several times, is heavily bandaged from the falls, and has become a pathetic sight indeed. She is still alive, however, when the narrator departs, having found out that his wasted friend "had finally one night decided to make it" with Tristessa, and "they made it, good," even though "Bull didn't rise to the issue except once every twenty years or so" (96).

The narrator "wanted some of that too," but he has "had some silly ascetic or celibacious notion that I must not touch a woman," even though his "touch might have saved her" (65). (How is not specified.) Evidently Kerouac has transferred to his narrator a vow of chastity, also referred to in *The Dharma Bums*, which was one of his heaviest investments in his transient Buddhism. Although the narrator falls in love with Tristessa, he is content to describe her as a saint and an angel.

One constantly gets the feeling that Kerouac has been searching for something that can qualify as a "long sad story" instead of discovering a situation that he comes to realize provides one. Two twists in the story line strengthen the suspicion that creating an effect is here more important than communicating an experience. The two parts of *Tristessa* may be wrapped chronologically around *The Dharma Bums* like crusts around a thick slice of bologna. At the beginning of the second part, in fact, Kerouac provides a capsule version of the novel yet to come that differs notably in tone from the final product. Instead of returning to Mexico the spring following the first episode, the narrator reports that he "went on to California and lived in a shack with young monk Buddhist type visitors every day and went north to Desolation Peak and spent a summer surling [sic] in the Wilderness, eating and sleeping alone" (63). The almost flippant way in which this narrator reports events that will later be invested with great solemnity indicates a vast difference between the points of view guiding the creation of the two novels and does indeed make *Tristessa* appear to be a counterpart of *Maggie Cassidy* in the works of Francis Martin, complementing the earlier springtime tale of a good/bad girl with this autumnal dirge about a bad/good girl.

This supposition is strengthened by an early passage in the book, in which the narrator confesses, "I wish my relatives in Lowell were here to see how people and animals live in Mexico—" (29). This remark paves the way for the celebration of the happy life of the Mexican poor, but it also suggests that the whole effort is intended at least in part to do what Kerouac achieved with so much more success finally than he had intended—shock smug American middle-class susceptibilities. Nearly everything in the book could serve this purpose, especially passages like one about an American tourist finding his treatment by some Mexican confidence men, "a case of wanting to be robbed, a strange kind of exultation and drunken power" (72).

This "innocents abroad" aspect of the book is summed up near the end by the narrator's lament, "My poems stolen, my money stolen, my Tristessa dying, Mexican buses trying to run me down, grit in the sky, agh, I never dreamed it could be this bad—" (84), but the book labors to prove that the nightmare of reality is even worse. ("Worse sensation in the world," we are informed, "to take morphine when you're drunk" [19].)

Tristessa may be called Kerouac's equivalent to Faulkner's *Sanctuary*, a deliberate effort to write the most shocking and sensational tale he could come up with in the hopes of attracting an audience. As such, the book works quite well, and it is surprising that it has not been more popular. It is likely that people hunting such slumming tales would not expect them from Kerouac, while, on the other hand, his fans could not appreciate a tale that is hard to take seriously.

Desolation Angels (1956–57, 1956 and 1961, 1965)

If *Tristessa* is Kerouac's most mannered performance, *Desolation Angels* is his most laidback, even though the writing of parts of them overlapped. Although Kerouac always refers to *Desolation Angels* as a novel, it is difficult to include this diary-like composite in such a generic term. Although real names are changed to those established as the dramatis personae for the Legend and although Kerouac, as usual, surely altered events and time sequences to suit his purposes, this book more than any other justifies Ginsberg's qualms about Kerouac's settling for writing travelogues and even Truman Capote's kittenish remark (long before this book emerged) about his works being "typing" rather than writing.

This is not to say that the book is not interesting. Indeed from the gossip's point of view, it is Kerouac's most readable and enlightening work, but it arouses interest as biography not art. It reels off in a seemingly unbroken strand (though there are demonstrable omissions), Jack Duluoz's experiences as the fictional stand-in for the novelist during the year between his last days as a fire watcher impatient to get back to civilization from Desolation Mountain in September 1956 to his ill-conceived plan to move his mother to a permanent abode in Berkeley, California, immediately before the publication of *On the Road* in September 1957. The action thus overlaps the last pages of *The Dharma Bums*, as well as the second part of *Tristessa*. Curiously in *Desolation Angels*, Tristessa is mentioned only once as one of Old Bull Gaines's drug suppliers; and there is no mention of the novel about her, as there is of other works—further evidence that Kerouac thought of *Tristessa* as a stylistic exercise outside the journal of his passing experiences.

The source of interest in *Desolation Angels* lies not in any perceptible artistic design, but in the offhand characterization of many of Kerouac's associates and the flashes of insight into his own increasingly depressed state of mind. At the opposite end of the creative spectrum from *On the Road*, the sum of the parts here greatly exceeds the impact of the whole.

Kerouac does make some ostentatious efforts to unify the book thematically, but he fails to sustain them. The first part of the book, describing Duluoz's reunion with the "Desolation Angels"—Cassady, Ginsberg, Gregory Corso, Peter Orlovsky, under their legendary aliases—in California after his lonely summer in the mountains in 1956, was written later that year when he was visiting Mexico, but he found no immediate market for it. After a long period of inactivity, following the writing of *The Dharma Bums*, when he returned to Mexico in 1961, he picked up where he had left off and wrote what he intended to be a separate book, "Passing Through," about his earlier return to the United States and his trip to Tangiers, Paris, and London. The two were combined only when Kerouac agreed with editor Ellis Amburn's suggestion to put them together for publication by Coward-McCann in 1965, when the beginning stirrings of anti-Vietnam activism had greatly diminished interest in Kerouac and the

Beat antipolitical stance. One would never guess that there had been such a long intervening break from the flawless way in which the first part flows into the second: either Kerouac's stylistic evolution had ended, or else he had settled on turning this entire work into a kind of norm from which his more arresting works were the departures.

His first effort to establish a pattern among the incidents occurs when Duluoz comes down from the mountain and discovers—the very first thing he notices—that in San Francisco "everybody was goofing—wasting time—not being serious—trivial in rivalries— timid before God—even the angels fighting" (66). This is the time when Ginsberg and others tried to interest Kerouac in poetic and po- litical causes, but found him disinclined to get involved. It is nearly a hundred pages later, however, before he realizes that he has "a big job on my hands patching things up" (150). He finally does find Ra- phael Urso (Corso) and Cody "in complete agreement" after a day at the races and compliments himself on having succeeded in his wait "to see them patch up and be friends" (169) The very point about "his wait," however, indicates the purely passive role he plays throughout much of this book in which he chronicles events without becoming substantially involved in them. "My life is a vast inconse- quential epic with a thousand million characters" (12), he observes near the beginning, and he maintains the same tone near the end when to the announcement that he, Irwin (Ginsberg) and Raphael are "now inseparably entwined in our literary destinies," he appends the ironic comment, "taking it to be an important thing" (200).

When he began writing *Desolation Angels* in 1956, the cynical Fran- cis Martin side of Kerouac's personality was clearly in control, so that he could feel a detached superiority to his quibbling friends. This, however, was before the publication of *On the Road.* He had suffered a terrible shock by the time he began "Passing Through" in 1961. Although the two accounts that were put together to make the book are stylistically consistent, there has been a drastic reversal in the nar- rator's state of mind. Early in the book contemplating "the void" from his lofty solitude on the mountain, he realizes that there is no place that "the bottomless horror of the world" (44) can be dis- pelled—including Lowell, New York, Frisco, North Carolina, China- town—and he now wants "a reproduction of that absolute peace" he found on the mountain "in the world of society" (219), but he takes this position with a feeling of serene superiority to the contending forces around him. He loses this feeling, however, when he gains celebrity: though looking back he realizes that naively, "I never dreamed I'd be taken in too by the world's actions" (220).

What the reader would now expect is an account of how he has been "taken in"; but this motif is not emphasized as we proceed in a leisurely manner through another string of vividly vignetted incidents, so that when his devastating discovery that he has been defeated by the world is revealed, it comes as a total surprise to the reader rather than as the anticipated culmination of carefully arranged incidents. We are told during an account of Duluoz's visit to Washington, D.C., to meet the official literary establishment that "I foresaw a new dreariness in all this literary success" (281), but this sounds only like the cynicism of the detached Francis Martin, who still sounds the dominating voice in Kerouac's pronouncements when he sneeringly observes that hipsters are becoming fashionable in Mexico City, but that "unlike American hipsters, they all have to go to work in the morning" (247).

Clearly Francis remains in control when at last Duluoz makes the long-deferred decision to go to Paris (even if now via Tangiers). Had Francis remained in charge, Kerouac could have become like his friend William Burroughs (Bull Hubbard in this novel) an expatriate. The trip, however, proves a devastating disaster that breaks Francis's hold and drives Duluoz back into the past. It begins with a fearful voyage on a Yugoslavian freighter through a storm that terrifies Duluoz despite his merchant marine experience. He explains that on this trip "the great change took place in my life which I called a 'complete turningabout' on that earlier page, turning from a youthful brave sense of adventure to a complete nausea concerning experience in the world at large, a *revulsion* in all the six senses" (300). There is a cry in his soul, "Why didn't I stay home?" With the subsequent revelation that as a result of an overdose of opium in Tangiers, he "actually got up and packed to go back to America and find a *home*" (303), a frame is provided that does unify the rest of the book, but we are now only sixty pages from the end of a long road.

The visit in Tangier proves worse than a disappointment—it is another bottomless horror. Unlike the travel-eager Irwin Garden (Ginsberg), who has a sightseeing itinerary ready for each new land that keeps his senses fresh and vital, Duluoz uses drink and dope to withdraw from these new scenes and even deeper into himself. Kerouac's Francis Martin personality has been attracted to visit Hubbard/Burroughs; and one would expect to find him delighted with his host's account of his new writings, "I'm shitting out my educated Middle-west background for once and for all. It's a matter of catharsis where I say the most horrible thing I can think of" (311), a technique that Kerouac had dabbled in when writing *Tristessa*; but instead of under-going the catharsis that will enable him to overcome his repressive past, Duluoz's overdose leads to an experience similar to that which Leo Percepied goes through at the critical point in *The Subterraneans*, as "that Virgin Mary headlight turning across the Bay headland sent streamer after streamer of salvation light over the picaresque of my ceiling," saying "Jack, this is the end of your world travel—Go home—Make a home in America. . . . The holy little old roof cats of silly old home town are *cry*ing for you, Ti Jean" (315). Peter Mar-tin (as the reversion to the name Ti Jean suggests) has reemerged and taken over, so that by the time Irwin Garden arrives to reinforce Francis, it is too late. Duluoz's friends protest his withdrawal, but he "couldn't explain it without telling them they bored me as well as everything else, a strange thing to have to say to people you've spent years with" (318). But then they would not really have known who was talking. So Duluoz—like Kerouac—rushes through Paris and London and back home.

By the time he comes to set down the account, Kerouac has re-gained enough balance to have Duluoz explain, "So I'd made that big trip to Europe at just the wrong time in my life, just when I became disgusted with any new experience of any kind" (330); but he makes clear that his life has been permanently changed when just before his last goodbye to his desolation angels, he introduces a long tribute to "the most important person in this whole story and the best," his mother, in which he berates those who seem to "hate" their mothers and praises "my quiet Sunday nights reading or writing in the privacy of my clean homey bed room" (334–36). So much for the Beats and the girls in New York and San Francisco that his mother had nothing to do with. The end of *Desolation Angels* does foreshadow the final choice of life-style that Kerouac himself will make.

Book of Dreams (1952–60, 1960)

Book of Dreams is exactly what its title announces, a collection of transcriptions of Jack Kerouac's dreams that, according to his fore-word, he scribbled down right after waking up, "spontaneously, non-stop, just like dreams happen." Clearly this is a cultist work, the interest of which lies not in the dreams, but in the dreamer; yet the book must be regarded as an essential part of the Duluoz Legend, since it provides often the kind of information that the writer has censored out in his conscious accounts of his waking moments. Dreams are as much a part of the life of an individual as the waking actions, and Kerouac often includes reports of dreams in other segments of the Legend, though none of these are repeated here.

The book, however, is difficult to fit chronologically into the Legend, because Kerouac dates only two of the dreams (in 1953 and 1954), rarely mentions where he dreamed them, and provides scarcely any helpful notes about the contents (although these could have been added later). Only occasionally does he even make the kind of judgment that he does near the very end of the book about a "STRANGE STRANGE DREAM of me making myself into a previous masturbating tape recorded body which lies right beside me whacking my hammer . . . " (Kerouac's ellipsis).[4] Even psychologists, oneiromancers, or other occultists would have difficulty providing illuminating commentaries on these reports, since we do not know even whether the dreams are reported in the order of their occurrence and what proportion of the total number of dreams over the unspecified period involved they represent. Many are also totally obscure fragments. Yet a few useful generalizations can be drawn from occasional passages that relate to incidents in Kerouac's other books.

Settings often change in middream and some identifications of places are ambiguous, so that it is difficult to formulate theories about the places to which Kerouac's dreams tended to take him back; the largest number are, however, set in the Lowell of Kerouac's childhood, indicative of a subconscious yearning for the past that figures largely also in his conscious writings. Most of the dreams, however, appear not to recall actual events, as they have no known counterparts in his early life. They appear rather an attempt to revamp it.

After Lowell, the next most frequent setting, especially early in the book, is Mexico City, suggesting the importance in his subconscious of this one foreign place to which he became attached over New York and San Francisco, with which he had much stronger and longer connections. Mexico City, however, was "abroad" for Kerouac, the furthest place from Lowell for which he developed any real feelings, though also the site of such disastrous experiences as Neal's desertion and the sad affair with Tristessa.

Several of the clearest and most intriguing dreams reveal feelings of guilt and inadequacy that Kerouac never allows to surface in his novels. The full impact of the disappointing reception of *The Town and the City*, followed by the failure even to find a publisher for *On the Road*, is suggested by his own appearance in one dream as "a thinner younger Major Hoople [a blowhard descendant of Dickens's Micawber, who was the central figure in a popular comic strip of the Depression years, *Our Boarding House*] who really had a small taste of early success but then lost it and came home to live off mother and sister but goes on 'writing' and acting like an 'author' " (32). His dreamself also appears as "a successful smiling New York Damon Runyon young genius writer (like the me of 1949)" (115–16); also he steals a pink wool sweater from outside a Jewish clothing store because he wanted "the middleclass security of pink wool sweaters" (30).

Not only does one get from these surfacings of inner perceptions a sense of the humiliation that depressed the aspiring writer during the 1950s, but also the reference to Damon Runyon, the popular, flashy, colloquial, but soon forgotten Broadway short story writer (best recalled for the tales that inspired the musical comedy *Guys and Dolls*) suggest that Kerouac conceived of himself as becoming a very different kind of writer from the cult hero that he finally became for the Beatniks. He records also his dreamself's "feeling guilty for writing *Doctor Sax, On the Road*, a sheepish guilty idiot turning out rejectable unpublishable wildprose madhouse enormities" (20), scarcely the view that one would expect from a writer inspired by James Joyce about his experimental work. "Somewhere there I took a wrong road," he admits in a dream (47), when he left Lowell for the life on the road. Kerouac's discontent with the figure he had become evidently began long before his withdrawal to Florida.

One of the most curious terms to surface in a dream does not appear to have been repeated elsewhere in his work. In a bleak flashforward to the future, he reports: "I'm married to Josephine and with all her friends around in the kitchen she makes fun of me and my 'writing' . . . a cuckold paramoured to a dike . . . a bleak laterlife with no balls, no joy, no Ma, no Kerouacism, nothing but the possibilities of the present ripened to full horror" (75–76). Whoever "Josephine" was (she is not identified in the glossary in *Jack's Book*) and whatever Jack himself thought about "Kerouacism" (the term suggests some kind of cult hero status), this is certainly the dream of a man who has been bitterly disappointed with life.

This impression is confirmed as an increasing number of visions of future wars begin to dominate his dreams. Doomsday images multiply, and he sees himself standing together with Irwin (Ginsberg) at Apocalypse (175). In the very last dream reported, "We're all prisoners of the Communists" (Cody is the only other person mentioned as present in the dream), where the only ones not suffering in agony are those kept in secret places by "women cooks & waitresses who need man-love so badly" that they "pay to be allowed to visit the hidden captive men-places to be laid" (183–84).

The very few dreams that are specifically described as "happy" pose even more puzzles than the horrible ones. In "Happy Dream of Canada," the usually nonpolitical Kerouac describes his dreamself's violent reaction to "a sarcastic freckled redhaired British Canadian." His "brother darkhaired anxious angry Canucks vehemently agree" with Kerouac. "Had I gone back to Canada," he continues, "I wouldn't have taken shit from any non Frenchman. . . . It was Ti Jean the happy Saint back among his loyal brothers at last" (118). Nowhere in his waking writings does Kerouac express such sympathy with the smouldering feelings of the French-Canadian separatists in Québec. What was the basis for this dream fantasy? If he did feel a strong sense of identification with the Québecois cause for which he never publicly fought, there may be another strand of subconscious guilt at work that would have to be considered in analyzing this troubled artist.

"The happiest dream" of Kerouac's life, however, takes him back to Lowell and his friends of the 1940s: "with Rudy Loval—I had been all around the world and away from Lowell, I was back, with Ma, in the 34 Gershom street house . . . of a Sunday morning everybody in Pawtucketville going to church—Rudy Loval as ever eager, warm—" (47). (The Kerouacs lived at 74 Gershom Avenue in 1941. Rudy Loval is not identified, but the name resembles Roland Salvas's.)

This glowing reference to "Loval," however, leads to one of the principal problems posed by *Book of Dreams*, the large number of references to intimate relationships with other men and especially the frequent references to "queers." This very derogatory term for homosexuals would have been by the time this book was published in 1961 considered as offensive an epithet as "nigger", but Kerouac is, of course, recalling the term embedded in his subconscious, and he uses it neutrally in the context of quite differing feelings. What is unexpected in this book, in view of Kerouac's attitudes expressed in his fiction, is the number of pleasant and favorable images of homosexual behavior. In *Desolation Angels*, Jack Duluoz states most emphatically, "I am a non-queer" (230), although Kerouac does also in that book for the first time publicly discuss Irwin Garden's (Allen Ginsberg's) public admissions of homosexuality and concedes that in Tangiers, "the creaks of pederast love" in a neighboring apartment didn't bother him (316).

There are a scattering of references in *Book of Dreams* to heterosexual relations, but these are surprisingly few and the first two deal with quite unromantic calculations about marrying an oil millionaire's daughter for her money (29). Later he watches a rich Jewish friend's sister "like a masturbator in the bathroom" and observes "I could have her and have millions but she'd never gave me a look" (33).

In the only real "sex dream" described, the narrator is not even sure of the identity of his companion: "Marie Fitzpatrick or somebody, and I, hot, go down the cellar stairs holding each others' organs" (117), and a final dream about undressing with Maggie Zimmerman focuses not on their relationship, but the way in which Jack uses it to shock "an old interfering fool" of an aunt (134).

Some of the dreams involving "queers" confirm Kerouac's assertion about his waking self. In one about a beautiful, blond Scandinavian boy, the whole male company present, except Jack, "wants to kiss him . . . on his erotic rosy lips" (18). Jack feigns innocence when a steward on the *S. S. Excalibur* makes an unwelcome pass at him under a desk (56); and in a dream about leaving Lowell for the city, he observes that in the city he finds "sodomists" chasing him, although he is also annoyed about "girls and women who tried to run my life" (48). In a more ambiguous early dream, he describes being "sought by the police also as a sex pervert because I have so much to do with young high school boys and girls while losing my pants" (19).

Most of the references to homosexual behavior, however, avoid such pejorative terms as "pervert" and present male relationships sympathetically. One of the first entries describes "a great unknown Greek writer, Plipias," who, when his father absconded with the family fortune, "went to live on an Island with the boy he loves" (9). Later, accompanying "some kind of Lil Abner Indian Buddy" to some kind of ritual party with "poor workingpeople," Jack thinks, "If any non Indians walked in here now they'd think it was a queer party" (59–60). Later he and Cody in a dream attend "a big queer party" in New Orleans, where Jack observes, "the queers seem to dislike us but I

dont really (in retrospect) believe they could have" (85). Later in an
account that many readers may find particularly distasteful, Jack talks
to Cody about an actor who is queer and finds himself excited "at the
mention of these erotic matters" (121).

At nearly the end of the book, the longest and most uncharacteris-
tic dream about homoeroticism is discussed at unusual length. Out
with Irwin and other buddies, in the dream Jack "realize[s] 'butch
drag' for the first time clearly" and sympathizes: "I'm kinda weird
myself, as I yell something at a group of girls and they come on dikey
with me on the boulevard." In the dream, he continues, "I'm a cul-
tured queer queen-king, part-saint, beloved—On waking it seemed
. . . I must have been a queer in that previous lifetime or couldn't
divine about 'butch drag' without experience in this lifetime" (176–
77).

The curious feature of these and other accounts is that in selecting
the material for this book, Kerouac did allow them to stand, although they might be interpreted as revelations of attitudes suppressed during his waking hours.[5] Perhaps in order to counter such
speculations, he at one point breaks into the account of a dream, as
he rarely does, to launch a vigorous blast against dream analysis, especially that with a Freudian basis: "dream-analysis is only a measure-
ment of the maya-like and has no value. . . . Dream-dispersion has
the only value—Freudianism is a big stupid mistaken dealing with
causes & conditions instead of the mysterious, essential, permanent
reality of Mind Essence" (158); but this protest seems quite strident
in the face of his willingness to publish the book, and one cannot
avoid the speculation that he may have been using this vehicle to un-
burden himself of troublesome problems that he could not face in his
fictions. He does not explain what he means by "dream-dispersion",
but his comments suggest that dreams arise from a continuing sensibility that transcends the separate incarnations of a spirit. Certainly
the differences revealed through this book between what Kerouac
sometimes dreamed and what he said in his wakeful moments suggest
again the kind of sharply divided personality that is embodied by his
fictional alter egos.

Indeed one of the most curious dreams of all is not collected in
Book of Dreams, but crops up suddenly in Kerouac's account of his
breakdown in *Big Sur*. After Jack reads some obscure fin de siècle poets, he naps and dreams of a navy ship anchored near a war scene:

"everything is drowsy as two sailors go up the trail with fishing-poles and a dog between them to go make love quietly in the hills: the captain and everybody know they're queer and rather than being infuriated however they're all drowsily enchanted by such gentle love."[6] The narrator comments only that the dream is "silly but strangely pretty"—perhaps the only "pretty" thing about the novel that will climax his career.

Chapter Nine
Breakdown—*Big Sur*

The wonder is not that following the unmanageable celebrity thrust upon Jack Kerouac by the success of *On the Road*, his work became increasingly fragmented and trivialized until he lapsed into four year's silence, but rather that after such a long period of despondency he was able to recover his bearings sufficiently to go on and write his most impressive and coherent novel as the capstone to the Duluoz Legend, even though he was able to do so only by driving himself to the verge of self-annihilation and then recovering enough to tell the story of the experience.

The Bixby Canyon Story

The narrator of *Big Sur* (1960, 1961, 1962) scarcely bothers to transform the author's identity at all, for he speaks of himself as the author of *On the Road* and other of Kerouac's works as he tells of his effort to find peace and quiet during a retreat in Lawrence Ferlinghetti's remote cabin in Bixby Canyon just off picturesque California highway 1, near the fashionable resort of Big Sur, during the summer of 1960.

Desperate to escape "the horror of literary notoriety," which has resulted in Kerouac's being "driven mad for three years by endless telegrams, phonecalls, requests, mail, visitors, reporters, snoopers,"[1] he had accepted Ferlinghetti's invitation to use the cabin to get away by himself for a while in July. Things did not, however, work out as they anticipated. Jack could not stand the ominous isolation of the foggy retreat, and before three weeks were over, he had hurried back to the city. He then moved twice more between San Francisco and the canyon, until on the night of 3 September he experienced a nervous collapse that drove him away from the canyon for good and, after a few days, back to New York. After this, he was to see little of his former California friends. In the novel Kerouac attempts to describe in harrowingly minute detail the course of his breakdown and to explore the causes of it.

The novel apparently follows the course of actual events with unusual fidelity, but since most biographical accounts have relied entirely upon the novel, we must remember that Kerouac's aim was to tell a story rather than to report an event journalistically. This caution is especially needed with this climactic work, for *Big Sur* is much more artfully structured than the rambling *Desolation Angels*. The artist is here more interested in communicating to the reader the feeling of such an experience, the process of the breakdown, than in an undeviating record of the events, and, as always in his narratives, he is trying to universalize his experience. *Big Sur* has a narrowness of focus and an intensity not to be found in most works based on Kerouac's life after the years mirrored in *On the Road* and *Visions of Cody*. The distinctive quality of *Big Sur* is that the reader is aware from the outset what the culmination of the events will be and that even the occasional digressions into verbal game-playing and philosophical speculation provide material essential for understanding the context in which the calamity occurs. The artist had, therefore, to be highly selective in choosing and arranging his materials—much more so than Kerouac had often been.

The narrative opens forebodingly with the description of the complete failure of an elaborate plot to keep Jack's visit to California secret (because of the unusual difficulty in distinguishing in this work between author and narrator, it is most satisfactory to use the first name that they share in recounting the novel). When, instead of heading directly for the hideout as planned, he blows his cover and disrupts the plan by calling up some friends for a drunken spree in San Francisco, he is forced to the realization that he has "hit the end of the trail and cant even drag my body any more even to a refuge in the woods let alone stay upright in the city a minute" (4). One senses that this is only the beginning of his troubles, even though he recovers enough, after having missed his promised ride to the canyon, to take a bus that brings him to Monterey at 2 A.M. and then a taxi costing eight dollars to Raton (as he redubs Bixby) Canyon.

On his arrival in chapter 3, he sounds the motif for the novel as he senses "something wrong somewhere" (9). What had seemed a lark to him back home in New York turns into "roaring mystery" in the Pacific darkness; and in a brilliant visualization of the state of mind that permeates the whole novel and even suggests the pattern of all his later years, he expresses the fear, as he begins the long, perilous descent from the highway into the canyon, that the railroad lamp that is his only guide, "will carry me astray if I dare to raise it for a minute from the ruts in the dirt road" (10).

In the morning he perceives what becomes throughout the book the symbol of his own plight—an "automobile that crashed thru the bridge rail a decade ago and fell 1000 feet straight down and landed upsidedown" (15). The view at the other end of the canyon is even more frightening and leads to Jack's parenthetically striking the note that provides the suspense to unify the narrative; he jumps ahead to point out that in six weeks "on the fullmoon night of September 3rd" (16), he would be going mad in this canyon, although he adds that he will never know the reasons, after some fine early days and nights in these "strange woods," his "soul so went down the drain" (19).

This pose of puzzlement is a rhetorical device, however, for he makes it clear what the problems on his divided mind are when he observes that "it's finally only in the woods that you get that nostalgia for 'cities' " (22) that only proves sickening. But despite enjoying "the most marvelous day of all when I completely forgot who I was where I was or the time of day" (28), he begins to get bored and feel that things are starting to go wrong on the fourth day. When he goes down to the ocean for a breath of good sea air, he gets an overdose of iodine, so that the sea seems to be yelling at him, "GO TO YOUR DESIRE DON'T HANG AROUND HERE" (41). When he foolishly decides he needs a trip to town, he has great difficulties hitchhiking and learns that the days on the road are over. He is also deeply upset by a letter from his mother informing him that his cat has died. After he collects some old buddies and starts drinking on a trip to visit Cody (Neal Cassady), Jack thinks he is seeing flying saucers and ends up in chapter 13 feeling "trapped" in "the grooky city" (70).

Although there are no formal divisions in this tight, fast-moving narrative of just over two hundred pages, the first thirteen chapters set the pattern for the book. With chapter 14 the drinking that continues throughout the novel begins in earnest with a nightmarish description of how the process that leads to delirium works (74–75). He does make his way back to the canyon, but this time followed by a pack of "observers" in a place where, as Lorenzo Monsanto (Ferlinghetti) observes, "a person should really be alone. . . . A big gang here somehow desecrates it" (94).

Jack begins to act peculiarly. When a party of friends luxuriate naked in some hot baths, neither he nor Cody will undress (though he reminds us that they are "supposedly the big sex heroes of our generation"), because "a gang of fairies" is watching, and he reports with horror seeing "spermatozoa floating in the hot water" (106–7). The next morning he awakens with the "final horrors" and a shockingly graphic description of delirium tremens follows (111–12). But even this episode is put into gripping dramatic perspective by chapter 21's concluding revelation that "the final horrible night" a week later will be even worse (114).

Jack's mental deterioration intensifies in what may be called the third movement of the novel (chapters 22–32), when he begins to wonder if his visiting friends "are all a big bunch of witches out to make me go mad" (115). Even his relations with Cody become strained later when Cody inveigles Jack into staying in San Francisco with Cody's new mistress. Jack begins to wonder if she and her friends, despite "fancy rigamarole about spiritual matters" may not be "a big secret hustler outfit" (152). He sinks into a virtually autistic state during the week that he spends in her apartment, "sitting in that same chair by the goldfish bowl drinking bottle after bottle of port" (157), until the seat collapses under him and he notices that the goldfish are dead. Cody's mistress Billie tries to persuade Jack to marry her, but her four-year-old son Elliott, whom Jack calls "one of the weirdest persons I've ever met" (148) does not like Jack. Despite this tension, Billie and Jack decide to persuade Dave Wain and his girl friend Ramona (based on Lew Welch and Lenore Kandel) to drive them and Elliott down to the canyon. Chapter 32 concludes with Jack looking forward bleakly to "the final horrible night" (175).

"It was actually such a gay night," he begins; but sounding again a motif for the book, he adds, "It always starts out good like that, the bad moments" (176–77). The bad ones come quickly enough when he determines to carry out his secret plan to confront Cody's wife with Billie. Although the meeting is uneventful, Cody refuses to say anything and this proves to be the last time that Jack sees either Cody or his wife. At the canyon, he realizes that he does not love Billie, "that I'm leading her on, that I made a mistake dragging everyone here, that I simply wanta go home now" (181). But this time there is no escape from the consequences of his drunken paranoia. Billie presses herself upon him during an afternoon session of love-making, while the four-year-old Elliott actually struggles to pull Jack off his mother. "It's the first time in my life I'm not confident I can hold myself together no matter what happens," Jack reports (187), and his suspicions of his friends increase until he decides that they are secretly trying to poison him, "because I'm a Catholic, it's a big anti-Catholic scheme, it's Communists destroying everything. . . . The drug is invented by Airapatianz, it's the brainwash drug" (203). He is beset by the notion that the Devil has come for him, but he concludes, "Suddenly as clear as anything I ever saw in my life, I see the Cross" (204). Although a last dreadful vision of a vulture haunts him, his traditional religion has come to the rescue again. He plans to return to his mother "and it will be golden and eternal just like that" (216).

Capping the Duluoz Legend

The ending of *Big Sur*, though hardly surprising in view of the similar redemptions by traditional religious visions at the ends of *The Subterraneans* and *Desolation Angels* is this time neither arbitrary nor unforeshadowed. It has been clear from the ominous opening of the novel that Jack is not capable of maintaining the isolation that dedication to artistic achievement would require. He is not, like James Joyce's alter ego Stephen Dedalus, a strong enough character to cast aside the nets that would restrain him. Nor are his friends, whom he systematically alienates, going to be able to aid him. Neither will his mother ultimately, even in the sheltered situation that she provides, be able to save him; but, for the time being, the struggle between the two contending forces has been resolved at last by his surviving the crisis that threatens to destroy him in the canyon. Peter Martin has at last won the victory over Francis and has even forestalled their joint self-destruction.

Duluoz/Kerouac has survived his supreme crisis and has lived to tell about it. Kerouac claimed to have written *Big Sur*, like *On the Road* and some other earlier works on a single teletype roll during ten days of maniacal typing in October 1961. That he clearly had the whole concept in mind is evidenced by the fast movement of the work and the unity of the text. The really remarkable thing about *Big Sur*, however, is the way in which in this final chronological installment in the Duluoz Legend, he made the deep split in his personality work once more to his artistic advantage for the first time since *Visions of Cody*. One of the clearest indications of his own at least partly conscious awareness of this split, after the conversation between the French-Canadian and English language voices within himself in *Visions of Cody*, occurs early in *Big Sur*, when the narrator is terrified by the dark road down the bluff, but " 'Follow the road,' says the other voice, trying to be calm" (11).

The difference between the cautious, traditional Peter born out of Kerouac's French-Canadian heritage, and the restless, alienated Francis, who developed out of Kerouac's cosmopolitan reading, is strikingly apparent here in the revelation that "the other" is always present, providing a counterbalance. This counterbalance works to the author's greatest advantage in *Big Sur*, because the most remarkable thing about the novel is not the grotesque record of an alcoholic breakdown that it presents, but Kerouac's ability to survive such a self-destructive experience and to describe it in a burst of creative energy that one would hardly expect after such an episode.

His personality was divided enough between his two "voices" that while his more volatile, uncontrollable self was succumbing to alcoholism and paranoia, his other self stabilized by deep family and spiritual roots was able to "follow the road," to watch and record with Kerouac's remarkable memory the details of the devastating experience. It could hardly be expected that an individual would be able to reconstruct in minute detail the disintegration of his own personality, but *Big Sur* provides such a record. Allen Ginsberg is exactly right when he describes the novel as "a heroic reconstruction of madness such as few dying men have ever reconstructed from hallucination & illness",[2] but apparently few critics have pondered the significance of Ginsberg's tribute, because he too often puffed works of Kerouac's that he had reservations about. This time, however, he delivered a definitive judgment of a great work of fiction.

Big Sur belongs to an important tradition of American writings that have never been widely popular, though they have usually at last commanded critical respect. Beginning with Charles Brockden Brown's *Wieland* and running through Melville's *Pierre*, Hawthorne's *The Marble Faun* (culminating a tendency in many of his short stories such as "Rappaccini's Daughter"), Henry James's *The Sacred Fount*, William Dean Howells's little-known *The Leatherwood God*, Harold Frederic's *The Damnation of Theron Ware*, Frank Norris's *Vandover and the Brute* and *McTeague* to Faulkner's *Light in August*, Steinbeck's *To a God Unknown*, Fitzgerald's *The Great Gatsby* and recently to all of James Purdy's novels from *Malcolm* through *Narrow Rooms*, American writers have been obsessed with characters bent on self-destructive courses who appear in glaring contradiction to the cherished "onward and upward" vision of the American dream.

Rarely, however, have these figures returned to tell the stories of their own crises. Usually the tale has been entrusted to an immensely involved, deeply disturbed spectator; only in Frederic's bitterly ironic novel is the central figure symbolically reborn to pursue another road to ruin. Even such American versions of the doppelgänger Jekyll-Hyde tales as Poe's "William Wilson" have usually ended in the violent destruction of both parties. Kerouac's model, however, if he followed one consciously at all, probably stemmed not from American sources, but from Dostoevsky or the poetry of Rimbaud that he so much admired. He did not need a literary model, however, for his tale of the nearly fatal struggle between the traditionalist and the "outsider" elements in a personality, because he had lived what he sought to fashion into Legend.

Why then did his effort come to no more than it did and why did he not produce other works that bring us so close to the verge of destruction as *Big Sur*? Once traditional forces had proved stronger and rescued him literally from himself, Kerouac was probably reluctant to tempt fate again. The only way in which he could have provided himself with raw materials for other works like *Big Sur* would have been to create deliberately situations like the one in which he found himself in California in 1960 in order to make a deliberate study of his own behavior (something that his once idol Thomas Wolfe tended to do). *Visions of Cody* indicates that Kerouac certainly had the imaginative capacity to engage in such a risky process, but only in *Big Sur* is the situation in which he is involved threatening enough to provoke a truly life-and-death crisis. He had been saved and sent "home" by visions of spiritual salvation before, after the experiences dramatized in *The Subterraneans* and *Desolation Angels*, but one of the inadequacies of these works is that the narrator's crisis is a trivial one that soon would have blown over and the "salvation" is melodramatically disproportionate to the necessity for it. There is little evidence, however, that Kerouac would have taken to the idea of turning himself into a guinea pig; he seems not to have realized when he took off for Bixby Canyon what he might be getting into, as he did to a certain extent when he went on the road with Neal Cassady or went to Tangiers to visit Burroughs.

Often in passing in his works Kerouac complains somewhat self-effacingly about his lack of guts. While he certainly had the guts to take chances that many others would not (especially during his days on the road), he probably refers to a cautiousness about sticking his neck out too far. He would not be likely again to expose himself to situations that would fuel another *Big Sur*, even if he had the physical and psychical energies left to confront them. *Big Sur* thus remains his unique contribution to an important American tradition. The novel has not yet received the recognition it deserves as an American classic, partly, one suspects, because such works upset readers and are slow to win an audience, and partly because, ironically, the author's celebrity has obscured the necessity for approaching the work as art rather than biography.

Satori in Paris (1965–66)

If the Duluoz Legend could ever be edited and published in a uniform edition—as would be the ideal arrangement—it would not end on the artistic high note or the psychological low note of *Big Sur*, but with an anticlimactic epilogue. Despite Kerouac's increasing withdrawal through the 1960s into an attempt to reconstruct the ambience of his childhood, he did set out on one more quest, embarking at last on the road to Paris, where he hoped to recover information about his presumably noble origins. This brief and, for the most part, disastrous junket provided the materials for the also quite brief *Satori in Paris*, published, unusually quickly for Kerouac's work, in July 1966 only a year after the trip. It is the last bit of his personal history that he would attempt to legendize.

The slight account might mercifully be passed over like some earlier sketches collected in *Lonesome Traveler* (1960), except that this time Kerouac decided to endow his memoirs with a special significance by introducing them with a high-toned lecture on the nature of literature. The function of literature, he asserts, is "to teach something of religious relevance." "Made-up stories about what should happen IF are for children and adult cretins who are afraid to read themselves into a book," he pontificates.[3]

The ostensible religious relevance of this work (which makes no pretense of being a novel) is that, as he states at the beginning, although he is uncertain of the source, "somewhere during my ten days in Paris (and Brittany) I had an illumination of some kind that seems to have changed me again, towards what I suppose'll be my pattern for another several years or more: in effect, a *satori*." The term, he explains is "the Japanese word for 'sudden illumination,' 'sudden awakening,' or simply 'kick in the eye' " (7).

The reader is thus alerted to expect some earth-shaking revelation that might help reshape his own life as well. *Satori in Paris* proves, however, to be an embarrassing example of the kind of moral fable (which Steinbeck also took to writing in his later years) that cannot stand up to the weighty burden that has been imposed upon it. The weakness of the work is not just that we soon learn that Kerouac is not at all sure when the satori occurred, but that he also cannot specifically identify what it was or what its religious relevance might be. He promises an illumination, but the lights never go on in the book.

Then beyond failing to clear up the confusion about just what his new pattern of life is going to be or why he is writing the book at all, the account, surely unintentionally, presents the narrator as a parody of the very people of whom he speaks condescendingly at the beginning. Kerouac launches into a familiar account of the common gaffes of American tourists that have strained our relations with the French. He then proceeds to run through his own repertoire of inadequately appreciating excellent dinners, complaining about the lack of facilities when he has failed to make advance arrangements, belittling the transportation and telephone systems, speaking contemptuously of contemporary French writers, and boasting, after he spends his first night with a gracious Frenchwoman of aristocratic origins, that she, of course, wanted to marry him, because "I am a great natural bedmate," as well, he modestly admits, as "a nice guy" (16).

Most pathetic, however, is his overinsistence on how well he has communicated with the French, not only in the language of Paris, but in the Breton dialect. He instructs a Jewish art dealer long resident in Paris in proper French pronunciation; and he comments in his most far-fetched effort to prove "what a miracle are different languages" that the French "couldn't have replied in detail to my detailed points if they hadn't understood every word I said" (46). He brags also about how well he was able to carry on a conversation with a Breton sailor who knew no English (62).

It never occurs to him that there is a difference between being able to talk to people correctly in their own language and having something to say to them. He presumed that because he could claim remote Breton ancestors, he would be welcomed with open arms by those with whom he had only distant connections, but his own experiences in Lowell seem to have taught him nothing about how a foreigner should behave in a provincial society. He apparently missed altogether the significance of a helpful tavern-keeper's comment that he should come back to Brittany again with his friends, or mother, or cousins (92).

During this episode, ironically, Kerouac does come up with what might indeed have provided the material for a satori when he observes that "it doesn't matter how charming cultures and art are, they're useless without sympathy" (88). He rushes past this remark, however, without apparently recognizing its application to his own overbearing behavior. His attempts to establish too quickly intimate rapport with a possible distant kinsman is probably, of course, not so much the result of insensitivity on Kerouac's part as of the anxiety engendered by the insecurity that is frequently the basis for clashes between cultures. "You always learn something and learn to change your thoughts, he observes at one point (43), but he does not. He quickly succumbs to homesickness and tries to find a consolation in drink that further exacerbates the bartenders, transportation workers, police officers, and postmen that he treats patronizingly.

The one thing that *Satori in Paris* clearly establishes as the winding down of the Duluoz Legend is that the Peter Martin voice in Kerouac is now firmly in control, as it probably has been since the moment of ecstatic redemption at Big Sur. The sophisticated, deracinated Francis, who longed to emigrate to Paris, has been completely overwhelmed by the childlike homebody Peter, who is no more comfortable in what he has come to fancy as his real home (Brittany) than most rural French-Canadians would be, so that Kerouac's long road ends at last in a hysterically hurried flight to the home that he had once left for what proved to be a dark and rutted road downward like the one into Bixby Canyon.

Chapter Ten
Kerouacism

So Jack Kerouac, alias Duluoz, reached his road's end in St. Petersburg, Florida, like so many of his fellow Americans. Most of these, however, have been "goldenagers" who have lived much longer than Kerouac, lives that have most infrequently been marked by the kind of excitement, turmoil, terrors, celebrity, and despair that his was.

The concrete bungalow that was his last home has not so far been designated as a literary shrine; nor is there a local monument to him. Should one be erected, what message might it bear to explain the reasons for Jerome Klinkowitz's observation that Kerouac's life had resisted his attempts at "literary legendizing"?

Before plunging into such speculations, one must emphasize that the kind of chronological pursuit of the Duluoz Legend undertaken here well repays the careful reader. If the tale that unfolds through the collected works can scarcely be said to skyrocket to the dazzling heights of legend, it does provide a unique case study of a kind of narcissistic person that many observers have found typical among mid–twentieth century Americans. Though not so different from many of his fellows as he fancied, Jack Kerouac was distinguished from the crowd by his seemingly uncanny gift of remembering everything that had happened to him, that had been said to him, that he had said himself, and by his recording whatever recollections he though appropriate while experimenting with various styles to find his proper voices.

To consider whether this confession merits the title of Legend, it is useful first to depersonalize the account and to compare the Kerouac/Duluoz Legend with a paradigm of the generic hero of traditional myth.

The Real Jack Kerouac and the Legendary Duluoz

Let us begin by imagining an extremely intelligent and morbidly sensitive man born into an ethnic minority group with its own language in a decaying city in a decaying region that had earlier been the industrial and cultural center of the country. The most profoundly disturbing experience of the man's childhood had been the death of his sickly but saintly older brother.

Going to school forces him to adopt the language of the mainstream culture, for which he displays an amazing facility, developing a large, often exotic vocabulary and fantastic writing speed. At thirteen he discovers the identity that will make him a face in the crowd through his athletic prowess, but even then he is inwardly more set upon becoming a creative writer. His athletic skills however, enable him to leave home for the big city, where he mingles with people who foster his artistic interests so that eventually he drops competitive sports to concentrate on his writing. When war comes, he proves unable to adjust to the discipline of either the military service or civilian marriage, but he takes a death-defying job in the merchant marine.

His most valued friend is killed in the war, and, casting about for a new life-style, the young man becomes involved with a group of malcontents who subsequently become the leaders of a new counterculture. He also becomes heavily involved in alcohol and drugs and faces the first crisis he cannot handle when he is inadvertently involved in a murder.

A psychologically troubling but artistically productive split in his personality becomes apparent when he attempts to forge an intimate relationship with a wild young man from the West, addicted to fast driving and free loving. He introduces our subject to the restless life on the road, but our subject spends only part of his time there and the rest at home with his mother trying to establish himself as a commercial writer. His first novel is published but quickly disappears from sight, and his subsequent work is for years considered too experimental for the publishing houses.

Home ties weakened, he drifts about, at the same time writing feverishly about his own experiences past and present, until at last a second novel is published and he becomes overnight a cult hero and the unwilling subject of a media publicity campaign. Unprepared by his background, education, or thirty-five years of neglect and obscurity for celebrity, he finds himself unable to handle it, loses control of his behavior, denounces his fans and friends, and stops writing for several years. Finally he experiences a partly alcoholic and partly spiritual breakdown from which he never really recovers, retreating instead more and more into trying to reestablish the milieu of his childhood away from the mainstream life of the culture that he has helped to change.

We may contrast this outline with what Joseph Campbell in *The Hero with a Thousand Faces* describes as "the nuclear unit of the mono-myth of the hero": "A hero ventures forth from the world of common day into a region of supernatural wonder: fabulous forces are there encountered and a decisive victory is won; the hero comes back from this mysterious adventure with the power to bestow boons on his fellow man."[1]

The Duluoz Legend falls far short of this pattern. The first part of the description of the hero's venturing forth from the ordinary to the supernatural world to win a decisive victory does describe *Doctor Sax*—Kerouac's most nearly "mythological" tale, but after returning from his adventures, Duluoz/Kerouac bestows few boons on his fellows and enjoys few triumphs himself. Beginning with *Maggie Cassidy* and extending through *Big Sur*, the Duluoz Legend recounts rather the disastrous misadventures of what was fashionably called during the mid–twentieth century an antihero.

Duluoz fails to qualify even for this title, however, for while there are scattered through the books of his Legend occasional attacks on the establishment like those in Allen Ginsberg's poem *Howl* and Ken Kesey's novel *One Flew over the Cuckoo's Nest*, Kerouac for years maintained a nonpolitical stance and then turned on the very Beat Generation that his writings had helped foster. In *Big Sur*, Duluoz's rescue from the inferno is not effected by a decisive personal victory but by a vision out of his traditional childhood religious background that sends him back to his mother and makes him in subsequent writings like *Desolation Angels* and *Vanity of Duluoz* harshly critical of the decadence of contemporary America. He never displayed transcendental powers after his fledgling flights in *Doctor Sax* and the world has not been restored as a result of his labors (as Campbell specifies the hero's must be). Duluoz/Kerouac simply escapes at the end of *Big Sur* from another unwanted marriage to hide in a retreat from which he can watch the world plunge into the Apocalypse he frequently dreams about.

A major reason that the Duluoz Legend is finally neither traditionally heroic nor fashionably antiheroic is the split in Kerouac's own psychical constitution between the conflicting voices that he embodied in his first published novel, *The Town and the City*, in the two

Martin brothers, Peter and Francis. We need in conclusion to review the shifting roles that these figures played in influencing his writing, especially as they struggled for dominance.

"Peter" and "Francis"

Peter is fashioned on young Ti Jean Kerouac, the preschooler who speaks only Quebecois and is deeply attached to his mother, sister, and saintly elder brother. As he grows, he becomes deeply rooted in his native soil, dreams of becoming a farmer, sympathizes secretly with the rebellious Quebecois in Canada, and remains deeply dependent on his domineering mother and his hometown friends, especially Sebastian, until the latter is killed in the war. As the years progress, Peter becomes increasingly introverted and fearful of change as he attempts to withdraw back into his childhood.

Francis, on the other hand, takes shape from that portion of Duluoz's mind and imagination that is inspired to break with what James Joyce called the "nets" of family, country, and religion by the creative sensibility that unites him in a common bond with other rebellious artists. He cannot accept any establishment ties or discipline, and he seeks to break away to become an expatriate. He is interested in experimentation in style and language and in seeking new sources of spiritual stimulation like Buddhism.

These two brothers are linked, however, by a common high intelligence and a common desire to write creatively. The struggle throughout Kerouac's life that he transfers to his alter ego Duluoz results from their contending efforts to hold the pen.

The Town and the City, with its praise of Lowell and country life, its toning down of many of Kerouac's most devastating experiences, and its assignment to Francis of the embarrassing episodes with Maggie Cassidy and the navy, is entirely Peter's book, written (in fact, greatly overwritten), during the intervals at home between the trips on the road with Neal Cassady in search of the "brother" to replace a lost twin, taken to appease the restless spirit of Francis. Kerouac apparently hoped that he might be able to establish himself as a writer within the framework of his family life, but his turning immediately upon completing this novel to the account of the road trips with Neal shows that Francis was taking over his imagination. The indifferent reception then further diminished hopes of making a reputation with Wolfean family chronicles in Peter's voice.

The "Cody" book, both in its three early versions and as *On the Road* and *Visions of Cody* becomes more and more Francis's work as third-person narration gives away to first and the downbeat ending of *On the Road* is replaced by the upbeat one of the Joycean tour de force *Visions of Cody*. Francis, now firmly in control and off in Mexico City, is responsible for *Doctor Sax*, the fantastic tale of his own creative liberation that ends on the most positive note of any of Kerouac's work and remains his most successful effort to turn his own experiences into legend.

From *Doctor Sax*, Francis speeds ahead to *Maggie Cassidy*, the next episode in Kerouac's life in which Francis's voice dominates in achieving a temporary liberation from Lowell and the possessive instincts of a woman who wants him to settle down. By this time, however, Kerouac's continuing failure to find publishers is weakening his self-confidence and undermining Francis's arrogant control. The next book about an unsuccessful romance, *The Subterraneans*, will become as it progresses distinctly Peter's, ending in a redeeming vision of the mother that will rescue him from the pit into which he has been dragged.

Possibly troubled by the see-sawing battle between the contending voices within him, Kerouac escapes in the mid-1950s for a while into Buddhist studies that provide him with a new model in Gary Snyder and a possible escape from both Lowell-bred "halves" of him and the hostile feelings of each towards the other's allies. The Buddhist release energizes Kerouac into a great spate of writing, but no really permanently significant works result; and when Kerouac is subjected to really serious trials, Buddhism fails to provide the resources necessary to carry him through them, so that he returns increasingly to traditional Catholicism. The Francis voice has meanwhile dominated *Tristessa*, his most cynical work and the only one that appears to have been written in a calculated effort to attract an audience with a sensational story rather than emphasize his own internal struggles. With *Visions of Gerard*, Peter's voice has surfaced again. By the time *On the Road* is published, the stabilizing influence of Buddhism is disappearing, and Kerouac is in the midst of an unresolved identity crisis even before he is demoralized by the notoriety that follows the publication of his novel.

His return to writing to try to produce a crowd-pleaser at his publisher's behest with *The Dharma Bums* ultimately disgusts him with potboiling, and he lapses into silence for four years, during which he undergoes, among other things, his breakdown in Bixby Canyon, out of which comes his last powerful work, *Big Sur*, which describes his final salvation through the triumph of Peter's voice and yearnings.

There follows only *Vanity of Duluoz*, Peter's final effort to expunge from the record the watered-down history and divided perspective of *The Town and the City* with a confession of his own failures and a running complaint against the decline of American character since his childhood. Kerouac had cut himself off from his old Beat buddies without appeasing those who had long been suspicious of his degenerate influence on youth and the national fibre. He had finally established Peter's voice as his own, but no one really cared. Francis, however, though defeated, could not be entirely suppressed, and Kerouac's excessive drinking during his last years could certainly have been prompted by voices still active within himself that he did not want to hear.

Peter Orlovsky characterizes the Kerouac of these later years with devastating and depressing accuracy when he says that during the Vietnam controversy, "Jack was taking the side of the rednecks."[2] This comment forces a recognition that Kerouac as Peter Martin had always been a redneck and that the efforts of "Francis" and "Doctor Sax," abetted by the Beat friends whom his mother detested, had never been able to marshall the strength to convert him for any length of time into a sophisticated intellectual.

The results of the shifts in points of view throughout Kerouac's fiction ultimately resulted in such an uneven body of work that it is unlikely he—especially in his St. Petersburg years—could ever have welded it into a consistent whole, even if he had had the energy to revise the whole account. The Legend, furthermore, lacks unity because of the omission of certain important phases of his life that he did not seem to want to write about. Little is said anywhere in his work about his two short-lived early marriages, and there is no substantial account of his relationship with Sebastian Sampas, although a parenthetical reference in *Visions of Cody* suggests that it may have been one of the most important in Kerouac's life and that Sebastian's death in the war may have been, of all the sad partings he had to experience, the most traumatic except for the childhood death of his brother Gerard.

Kerouac as Rimbaud and the Lost Verlaine

Into his accounts of what have usually been considered his closest mature male relationships with Neal Cassady and Allen Ginsberg in

Visions of Cody, Jack inserts, parenthetically, a most unusual and unparalleled flight of metaphor: "(like Rimbaud and his Verlaine, every
rose's got a summer, Julien and his Dave, I had my Sebastian: Julien's
Verlaine was murdered, my Verlaine was killed in a battle of war,
Cody's Verlaine though is Irwin—or was—."[3] Kerouac makes no such
comparison anywhere else in his writings, but this certainly raises
questions about the nature of his relationship with Sebastian. Before
pondering these, however, we need to clarify the text.

We need not dig back into histories of the French symbolist poets
to learn about the actual relationship between Rimbaud and Verlaine
that provides the vehicle for Kerouac's metaphorical presentation, because Kerouac presents his own version of the earlier poets' relationship in a 1959 poem. Lamenting the waste of a gifted but
unsophisticated boy from the provinces at the hands of a decadent literary clique in the big city, Kerouac wrote in part:

> Heaven is everywhere
> Nevertheless the old fags intervene . . .
>
> Verlaine summons to Paris
> with less aplomb than he
> did banish girls to
> Abyssinia
>
> "Merde" screams Rimbaud
> at Verlaines salons
> Gossip in Paris—Verlaines wife
> is jealous of a boy
> with no seats to his trousers.[4]

Finally in a fit of passion Verlaine shoots Rimbaud and is jailed.

Although Kerouac had been aware of Allen Ginsberg's homoerotic
propensities since Ginsberg had come out in the 1940s, Kerouac was
unwilling or unable to acknowledge them in his fiction until 1961
(except for this strange parenthesis in *Visions of Cody* to understand
which the reader would need a key). The passage here refers to a situation early in the friendships of Kerouac, Ginsberg, and Cassady,
when the latter pair engaged in homosexual encounters, with Cassady
playing a passive role until he tired of the whole business (hence the
final "was" in the *Cody* passage).

Julien is the alter ego of Lucien Carr, Kerouac's chum at Columbia

University during World War II, who had murdered David Kammerer, a former teacher who had been pursuing Carr in an attempt to force a homosexual relationship upon an unwilling Carr. Thus the three comparisons that Kerouac introduces in *Visions of Cody* to his own relationship with Sebastian all refer to aggressively homosexual pursuers of unwilling or unenthusiastic young men.

Kerouac's identification of himself with Rimbaud is easily understood as a somewhat exaggerated self-dramatization as an unsophisticated boy from the country seduced into the evil big city world of drugs and drink. But what had hometown friend Sebastian to do with such an image? What is the point of this extended analogy?

Sebastian Sampas was the younger brother of Stella Sampas, who became Kerouac's third wife near the end of his life. In *Visions of Cody*, Jack departs from his customary fictional practice by using Sebastian's real name as well as David Kammerer's, possibly because both were dead and could not protest, but possibly also because he had in mind other similarities between them.

The development of Jack's friendship with this boy of Greek ancestry is dramatized principally in Kerouac's first novel, *The Town and the City*, in which the division of his own experiences between Peter and Francis Martin occurs. Although Peter and Alexander Panos, as the character based on Sebastian is named in the novel, have lived in the same town since childhood, they become acquainted only during the summer of 1940 when Peter returns from prep school before Columbia—after he has begun his literary career by publishing some fiction in the school magazine. Peter does not remember meeting Alexander before, but Alexander remembers Peter as the boy who with an older brother Joe (who has no real life counterpart) had defended the eleven-year-old Greek (not normally an ally of the French-Canadians) from Irish bullies. Peter's old sidekicks are suspicious of Alexander, but he becomes "a great friend" of Peter's, "a comrade, a confidante in the first glories of poetry and truth." Panos was the first boy Peter knew who was interested in books and who spoke of "ideals," "beauty," and "truth." "They often argued because there was a powerful division in their personalities and backgrounds and upbringing that could have separated them before their friendship could grow. But . . . Alex was always aware of the underlying tenderness and understanding in Peter himself" (137).

Peter's brother Francis, however, cannot stand "that awful Greek" of Peter's (191),[5] although he later regrets not befriending him when

Alex writes him a pathetic letter about army experiences. Meanwhile Peter and Alex have seen each other for the last time just before Peter ships out with the merchant marine. When the news of Alex's death in battle reaches Peter, "It was as though something had broken inside him, all fallen and ruined" (439).

The relationship between Peter and Sebastian is one of the major events of Kerouac's life to which he was able to return fictionally for rewriting when late in life he replaced *The Town and the City* with *Vanity of Duluoz*. Again they meet in the summer of 1940; but this time Sabby Savakis, as he is now called, definitely pursues Jack and pushes the beginning of their friendship, when he says that since his rescue from the bullies, he has always wanted to talk to Jack. When Jack asks rather crudely, "What the hell you want to see me for?" Sabby replies, "No particular reason. Been watching you."[6] Although they see little of each other that summer, Jack describes Sabby as "everything a man should want as a friend" (63).

Their last meeting is much more vividly portrayed than in *The Town and the City*, and their conversation is exceptionally sentimental, ending with Jack's recollection of his departure from Lowell for prep school in 1939, when Sabby ran alongside the departing train singing "I'll See You Again," Noel Coward's classic evocation of the painful parting of lovers (163–64). Then Jack reports abruptly that Sabby was killed at Anzio beachhead in Italy and launches into an impassioned attack, rare in his fiction, blaming the disastrous battle on General Mark Clark's ambitions, for which Jack hopes "he may be damned for the dead of Salerno" (164).

The report of Sabby's death has reached Jack just at the time he is being observed for a psychiatric discharge from the navy. On a short train trip between hospitals, he observes that he "took the opportunity to fantasize, or that is, to relieve myself of the horror of masculinity. 'Heart' and 'kiss' is only something's sung by gals" (166).

Kerouac must have realized that his handling of the elaborate Rimbaud/Verlaine analogy in *Visions of Cody* implied an homoerotic element in his relationship with Sebastian, and his angry and frustrated reflections on Sabby's death suggest a stronger feeling than customary male bonding. One only wonders what might have happened had Sebastian Sampas survived the war, since he was the kind of "angelic friend" that Kerouac failed to find in demonic Neal Cassady. Kerouac, in fact, never again established the kind of relationship that he had with Sebastian, and when at the end of his life he realized that he needed a kind of affectionate caretaker for himself and his mother, he turned to Sebastian's sister Stella. Had Sebastian survived, could he have managed to integrate the "Peter" and "Francis" voices in Kerouac and introduce into Jack's life the kind of stability that it lacked after Sebastian's death?

"Guts" and "Joy"

Jack recognizes a principal element contributing to this instability when, during an exhausting climb back down a mountain in *The Dharma Bums*, he attributes to his alter ego Ray Smith the feeling that despite his friend Japhy's urging, he cannot go on. "In fact," he observes in one of the most candidly self-revealing remarks anywhere in his fiction, "I realized I had no guts anyway, which I've long known. But I have joy" (72). This bit of self-analysis comes as a jolt to any reader who has been following Kerouac's fictional reincarnations since *On the Road*, for he has seemed to display considerable guts in the chances that he takes with Cassady's wild driving, in bouts with drinks and drugs, in sailing with the merchant marine into submarine-infested waters during the war.

He is quite right, however, that when it comes to personal confrontations, he often lacks the internal resources to resolve his own problems heroically. In *The Subterraneans* and *Desolation Angels*, as finally most forcefully in *Big Sur*, personal crises of increasing severity are resolved only by a literal deus ex machina in his visions of his mother and the Cross. Even his playing Russian roulette with himself in adventures on the road is not so much an example of a will to survive as of the kind of suicidal complex to which Kerouac ultimately succumbed in St. Petersburg. It is not "the guts" to face death that he lacks, but the guts to face life and the "forlorn rags of growing old."[7]

But how can this complex be reconciled with his further claim in *The Dharma Bums* to having "joy"? There is little joy in the common meaning of the term in *Maggie Cassidy*, *Tristessa*, *Desolation Angels*, *Big Sur*, or *Vanity of Duluoz*, little joy even in the apocalyptic visions of the *Book of Dreams*. Kerouac observes in *Big Sur* that the bad moments always start out good; the same observation might be made of his journeys to Mexico City, Tangiers, and Brittany. The "joy" in *The Dharma Bums* itself is limited to the bacchanalian moments when Ray Smith drinks enough to overcome his inhibitions.

This joy seems to be found only in those fleeting moments when Kerouac or his various alter egos are transported out of the valley of sorrows by listening to favorite jazz musicians or during the few electric minutes before the pot takes over and the conversation drifts into incoherence in the tape recordings transcribed for *Visions of Cody*. Such joy is a very fleeting and fragile thing. No wonder that Kerouac could never really give himself up to Buddhist teachings as Gary Snyder did and stop drinking as Snyder pleaded with him to do. Joy to Kerouac was the spirit of carnival that required and allowed external stimulation before the dark repentance of the Lenten season.

The key to understanding this concept cannot be found in Kerouac's work; but one of its best fictional embodiments is found at the end of John Steinbeck's early novel *To a God Unknown*, when the drought that seems to have doomed a rural valley in California is broken and the Mexican-American (Kerouac's beloved fellaheen) rejoice. A priest listens to them: "[He] could see in his mind how the people were dancing, beating the soft earth to slush with their bare feet. He knew they would be wearing the skins of animals, although he didn't know why they wore them. . . . 'They'll be taking off their clothes,' the priest whispered, 'and they'll roll in the mud. . . They'll be rutting like pigs in the mud.' " His description fits some of the festivities in *The Dharma Bums*, which Ray Smith, despite his claims of "having joy," could never quite join. "They wanted the rain so, poor children," the priest goes on. "I'll preach against them on Sunday. I'll give everybody a little penance."[8]

Kerouac had been indoctrinated during his childhood with this same conception that the unrestrained expression of joy, this reversion to pagan ways, is a release valve from the tensions of life that must be paid for with long periods of repentance. The concept of joy as a permanent state of serenity achieved through meditation is something that Kerouac never really grasped. He was too deeply imbued with the French-Canadian peasant conception of suffering through a hard week's work to find explosive relief in a riotous Saturday night, followed by a physical and spiritual hangover on Sunday.

This belief was further complicated by his childhood exposure to New England's work ethic. In *On the Road*, in a fleeting moment of joy, he does see Dean as "the pagan mayor of San Francisco," but he observes sadly that his energies ran out. Joy demands too much energy to sustain itself in the human condition. Ultimately, Kerouac's vision of life is best encapsulated in Duluoz's comment in *Big Sur* as he begins his midnight descent into the valley where he will experience his supreme crisis, "I actually fear that even my lamp will carry me astray if I dare to raise it for a minute from the ruts in the dirt road" (10).

Duluoz/Kerouac's eyes are rarely raised to the sun as they are at the end of *Visions of Cody*. Although Kerouac's vision of "the road" in *On the Road* has become identified with him, it is only a fleeting perception. His road is less often the concrete ribbon of escape than the rutted dirt path that must be perilously followed with a faint lamp. Only in his travels with Doctor Sax does the narrator of the Duluoz legend achieve the transcendence of the ordinary human condition that is expected of the hero.

Even upon brief acquaintance the astute Gore Vidal was better able to put his finger on Kerouac's essential character than many who had known Jack longer, when he observed that Kerouac was "basically timid."[9] This timidity was evidently very appealing to those who knew him personally as someone in need of protection. Philip Whalen speaks for many others when he observes that "everybody loved Jack,"[10] a judgment that one reading his books sometimes finds puzzling. He evidently had some kind of personal magnetism that, despite the techniques he experimented with to try to achieve immediacy in his writings, he rarely—perhaps only in *On the Road*—succeeded in infusing into his work. Perhaps we need look no further for the reasons that he failed to legendize his life and that the story of his life remained more intriguing to many than his writings.

On the Road has, however, appealed and continues to appeal to several generations of readers. Probably a principal reason is that many, like Kerouac, who have started out with the high aspirations he dramatizes in *Doctor Sax*, have shared enough of his kind of experiences to identify with the defeatist conclusion of *On the Road*. It is a great consolation for losers, but to stay with a writer through a lifetime's quest an audience devoted to its own quests requires a more inspiring model.

Julian Moynahan may have provided in 1968, just before the end of Kerouac's career, the best brief summary of his achievement that remains valid today: "*On the Road* retains a substantial period charm but most subsequent books that I have read are spoiled by logorrhoea and shapelessness. *Dr. Sax* is an exception to this statement but *Satori in Paris* is a disastrous illustration of it."[11]

Three decades after its publication, *On the Road* is indeed an enduring period piece, probably the most successful of its time, but it is also something more. It achieves the universality that Kerouac sought in all his work, but only if it is perceived truly as a cautionary tale rather than the promotional tract it has been taken for, usually by careless readers or nonreaders. Moynahan may not have been familiar with the long elusive *Big Sur*, but it is one of the most personal and remarkable of many accounts of the crack-up of an individual for whom the world has begun to move too fast and his redemption through a self-abasing return to the traditional certainties of childhood. Kerouac in the end did not succeed in creating a Legend, but he has provided us with a remarkable case study of Kerouacism.

Notes and References

Preface

    1. See Tom Clark, *Jack Kerouac* (San Diego: Harcourt Brace Jovanovich, 1984), 170.
    2. Letter to Ellen Lucey, 14 January 1950. (Information supplied by Tim Hunt.)
    3. Quoted in Barry Gifford and Lawrence Lee, *Jack's Book* (New York: St. Martin's Press, 1978), 271.

Chapter One

    1. *Heaven & Other Poems* (Bolinas, Calif.: Grey Fox Press, 1977), 39–40.
    2. Tom Clark, *Jack Kerouac* (San Diego: Harcourt Brace Jovanovich, 1984), 3.
    3. Ibid.
    4. Kerouac's native tongue is generally called Québécois; but Clark explains (ibid.) that it should be properly called *Joual*, a term which he identifies as "coined in the 1950s" to describe an "Anglicized, abbreviated, and musical form of French spoken by the Quebecois of the St. Lawrence Valley."
    5. *On the Road* (New York: Viking Press, 1957), 148.
    6. Stanley Aronowitz, "Voice Literary Section," *Village Voice*, 7 May 1985, 13.
    7. Clark, *Kerouac*, 22.
    8. Ibid., 21; *Doctor Sax* (New York: Grove Press, 1959), 148.
    9. *Vanity of Duluoz* (New York: Coward-McCann, 1968), 50.
    10. *Two Early Stories* (New York: Aloe Editions, 1973).
    11. Charles E. Jarvis, *Visions of Kerouac* (Lowell, Mass.: Ithaca Press, 1974), 91.
    12. *Heaven & Other Poems*, 39.
    13. Clark, *Kerouac*, 84.
    14. Letter to Allen Ginsberg, 5 July 1949. (Information provided by Tim Hunt.)
    15. *Heaven & Other Poems*, 39.
    16. Ann Charters, *Kerouac: A Biography* (San Francisco: Straight Arrow 1973), 174.
    17. Letter to Neal Cassady, 10 January 1953. (Information provided by Tim Hunt.)
    18. Gifford and Lee, *Jack's Book*, 188.

19. See Lawrence Ferlinghetti, "Horn on 'Howl,' " *Evergreen Review* 4 (1957): 145–58 for a summary history of the obscenity trial and Judge Clayton Horn's decision for the defendants.

20. Editor Martha Foley subsequently selected the story for inclusion in *Best Short Stories of 1955* (Boston: Houghton Mifflin, 1956), bringing Kerouac his first establishment literary recognition.

21. *The Scripture of the Golden Eternity* (New York: Totem Press, 1960), unpaged.

22. Gifford and Lee, *Jack's Book*, 217.

23. Clark, *Kerouac*, 153.

24. *Heaven & Other Poems*, 39.

25. Information provided by Tim Hunt.

26. Clark, *Kerouac*, 165.

27. Introduction to *Beatitude Anthology* (San Francisco: City Lights, 1960), 3.

28. Ibid.

29. Quoted in Gifford and Lee, *Jack's Book*, 277.

30. See Jarvis, *Visions of Kerouac*, 1–8, for the most thorough account of the importance of *Visions of Gerard* to Jack Kerouac. Jarvis argues that "Kerouac never doubted that Gerard fashioned the great riffs that are Kerouac's novels" (7). Some critics are skeptical, but the report seems sound.

31. Tom Wolfe, *The Electric Kool-Aid Acid Test* (New York: Farrar, Straus and Giroux, 1968), 90.

32. I am following here Tom Clark's statement in *Jack Kerouac* that sister Nin "suffered a fatal coronary occlusion" (201).

33. Stella Sampas told Gifford and Lee that Jack had asked her to marry him before he married Joan Haverty, but she had refused because of obligations to her family (*Jack's Book*, 304). For a local account of Kerouac's relationships with the Sampatacacus family—as the Sampases were originally named, see Jarvis, 51–74.

34. *City Lights Journal* 4 (1978): 246.

Chapter Two

1. *New Yorker*, 25 March 1950, 115.

2. Thomas Wolfe, *Look Homeward, Angel* (New York: Charles Scribner's Sons, 1929), 491.

3. *Book of Dreams* (San Francisco, City Lights Books 1961), 17.

4. Letter to Ellen Lucey, 14 January 1950. (Information supplied by Tim Hunt.)

5. *The Town and the City* (New York: Harcourt, Brace, 1950), 135. Subsequent page references in the text.

6. In "Jack Kerouac Biography," *Heaven & Other Poems*, 51, Kerouac speaks of reading Saroyan when he was eighteen and of "writing terse little stories in that general style."

7. John Clellan Holmes, *Go* (New York: Scribner's, 1952), 10. Subsequent page references in the text.
8. Holmes, *Go* (1952; reprint ed., Mamaroneck, N.Y.: Paul A. Appel, 1978).

Chapter Three

1. Allen Ginsberg and Allen Young, *Gay Sunshine Interview* (Bolinas, Calif.: Grey Fox Press, 1974), 3.
2. Charters, *Kerouac,* 223.
3. Clark, *Kerouac,* 152.
4. *On the Road,* 91. Subsequent page references in the text.
5. "After Me, the Deluge," *Chicago Tribune,* 28 September 1969, Sunday Magazine, 3. The article was also syndicated to other newspapers, where it appeared under various titles.

Chapter Four

1. Dates given in subheadings in this chapter identify first the date of the writing and second the date of the publication of the work.
2. *The Subterraneans* (New York: Grove Press 1958), 85–86. Subsequent page references in the text.
3. John Updike, "On the Sidewalk: (After Reading, At Long Last, 'On the Road,' by Jack Kerouac)," *New Yorker,* 21 February 1959, 32.
4. Quoted in Gifford and Lee, *Jack's Book,* 183. Vidal criticizes Kerouac for not going on in the novel to show the two characters going to bed together. Kerouac claimed he had "forgotten," but when Vidal challenged this explanation, Kerouac replied, "Maybe I wanted to forget."
5. Charters, *Kerouac,* 186.
6. Ibid., 185.
7. Clark, *Kerouac,* 166.
8. Ibid., 183. Ginsberg's review appeared in the *Village Voice,* 12 November 1958, 3–5.
9. This mountain in Marin County is pictured on the cover of John Montgomery's *Kerouac West Coast* (Palo Alto, Calif.: Fels & Firn, 1976).
10. *The Dharma Bums* (New York: Viking Press, 1958), 89–91. Subsequent page references in the text.
11. *Heaven & Other Poems,* 40.
12. Tim Hunt, *Kerouac's Crooked Road* (Hamden, Conn.: Archon Books, 1981), 100.
13. Ibid., 102–3.
14. *Pic* (New York, 1971), 78. Subsequent page references in text.
15. Hunt, *Crooked Road,* 104.
16. Ibid., 101–2.

Chapter Five

1. *Vanity of Duluoz* (New York, Coward-McCann, 1968), 195.
2. *Visions of Gerard* (New York, 1963), 145. Subsequent page references in the text.
3. Dates following the separate books constituting the Duluoz Legend identify: (1) the period in Kerouac's life on which the book is based, (2) the date of composition, (3) the date of publication.
4. Jarvis, *Visions of Kerouac* 1–8.
5. Ibid., 7.
6. He was never able to make any headway on a Proustian account of Lowell life to be called *Memory Babe* (see Clark, *Kerouac*, 166).
7. *Book of Dreams*, 102.
8. *Doctor Sax* (New York: Grove Press, 1959), 97. Subsequent page references in the text.
9. Clark, *Kerouac*, 120.

Chapter Six

1. "In the Ring," *Atlantic Monthly*, March 1968, 100.
2. *Vanity of Duluoz*, 26. Subsequent page references in the text.
3. *Maggie Cassidy* (New York: Avon Books 1959), 178. Subsequent page references in the text.

Chapter Seven

1. Hunt, *Crooked Road*, xvii.
2. Ibid., 85.
3. Ibid., 94.
4. Ibid., 90.
5. Ibid., 114–15.
6. Ibid., 120.
7. Letter of 3 July 1952, quoted in Hunt (140) at greater length as Ginsberg expresses doubts that the work can be published and speculates about Kerouac's condition.
8. *Visions of Cody* (New York: McGraw-Hill, 1972), 3. Subsequent page references in the text.
9. Hunt, *Crooked Road*, 231.
10. Ibid., 249.
11. Ibid., 237.
12. Ibid., 210, 223.
13. Because it was irrelevant to his purpose of explicating Kerouac's intentions and achievement in the several versions of the work that culminated in *Visions of Cody*, Tim Hunt properly pays no attention to this abridged version of the novel in *Kerouac's Crooked Road*. Since also the

abridgement appeared in a limited edition that has now become a collector's prize, so that few will ever see it, extended comparison of it with the original serves no purpose. Briefly, little is used from the first part of the novel and the tapes and the imitations of them are almost entirely dropped. About one-third the length of the original, the abridgement includes principally scenes from the second part about Cody's teenage years in Denver, the central "visions of Cody," and the final pages of the book. Even the shorter version of the material covered in *On the Road* in the last part of the book is omitted, probably because it might have seemed to duplicate that novel, though it does not.

14. Hunt, *Crooked Road*, 251.

15. *Old Angel Midnight* (London: Midnight Press, 1985), section 4, unpaged.

Chapter Eight

1. *Desolation Angels* (New York: Coward-McCann, 1965), 221. Subsequent page references in the text.

2. *Tristessa* was written in two parts, each immediately following the events fictionalized during the summers of 1955 and 1956 in Mexico City.

3. *Tristessa* (New York: Avon Books, 1960), 33. Subsequent page references in the text.

4. *Book of Dreams*, 182. Subsequent page references in the text.

5. Kerouac did permit at least one change in the text of *Book of Dreams*. In a letter to publisher Lawrence Ferlinghetti (25 May 1961), he agreed to substitute "boffing" on page 184 for an obscenity that might have gotten the book banned (information from Tim Hunt).

6. *Big Sur* (New York: Farrar, Straus & Cudahy, 1962), 119.

Chapter Nine

1. *Big Sur*, 4. Subsequent page references in the text.

2. Letter to Dennis McNally, 23 March 1978, quoted in Robert J. Milewski, Jack Kerouac: *An Annotated Bibliography of Secondary Sources, 1944-1979* (Metuchen, N.J.: Scarecrow Press, 1981), 202.

3. *Satori in Paris* (New York: Grove Press 1966), 10. Subsequent page references in the text.

Chapter Ten

1. Joseph Campbell, *The Hero with a Thousand Faces* (Cleveland: Meridian, 1949), 245.

2. Quoted in Gifford and Lee, *Jack's Book*, 303.

3. *Visions of Cody*, 345.

4. *Rimbaud* (San Francisco: City Lights Books, 1960), unpaged broadside. The poem had originally appeared in 1959 in Leroi Jones's magazine *Yugen* 6.

5. Francis's comment is an extraordinary example of a disagreement between two characters, both of whom were based on Kerouac himself, showing the kind of mixed love-hate feelings that he must have had about some of the people closest to him. The disagreements between Peter and Francis foreshadow the debate over Cody in *Visions of Cody*.

6. *Vanity of Duluoz*, 60. Subsequent page references in the text.

7. *On the Road*, 254.

8. John Steinbeck, *To a God Unknown* (New York: Robert O. Ballou, 1933), 237.

9. Quoted in Gifford and Lee, *Jack's Book*, 183.

10. Ibid., 219.

11. Julian Moynahan, "Twenty Beat Years," *The Listener*, 27 June 1968, 841.

Selected Bibliography

PRIMARY SOURCES

Only separate publications (books, pamphlets, broadsides) are listed. The works considered in this book as components of the Duluoz Legend are marked with an asterisk (*).

1. Novels
* *Big Sur*. New York: Farrar, Straus, & Cudahy, 1962.
* *Desolation Angels*. New York: Coward-McCann, 1965.
  The Dharma Bums. New York: Viking Press, 1958.
* *Doctor Sax: Faust Part Three*. New York: Grove Press, 1959.
* *Maggie Cassidy*. New York: Avon Books, 1959.
  On the Road. New York: Viking Press, 1957.
  Pic. New York: Grove Press, 1971.
  The Subterraneans. New York: Grove Press, 1958.
  The Town and the City. By John Kerouac. New York: Harcourt, Brace, 1950.
* *Tristessa*. New York: Avon Books, 1960.
* *Vanity of Duluoz: An Adventurous Education, 1935–46*. New York: Coward-McCann, 1968.
* *Visions of Cody*. New York: McGraw-Hill, 1972. Introduction by Allen Ginsberg. (Excerpts from the novel were published in a limited edition with the same title—New York: New Directions, 1959.)
* *Visions of Gerard*. New York: Farrar, Straus, 1963. Illustrated with drawings by James Spanfeller.

2. Short Fiction
  The Great Western Bus Ride. London: Pacific Red Car, 1984. (Possibly a selection deleted from *On the Road* that originally appeared in *Esquire*, March 1970.)
  Home at Christmas. London: Pacific Red Car, 1984.
  Two Early Stories. New York: Aloe Editions, 1974. ("The Brothers" and "Une Veille de Noel.")
  Two Stories. London: Pacific Red Car, n. d. (Contains "The Rumbling, Rambling Blues" and "In the Ring.")
  The Vision of the Hooded White Angels. London: Pacific Red Car, 1985.

3. Miscellaneous Autobiographical Prose
* *Book of Dreams.* San Francisco, City Lights Books, 1961.
  Lonesome Traveler. New York: McGraw-Hill, 1960. Illustrated with draw-
      ings by Larry Rivers. (Contains "Piers of the Homeless Night,"
      "Mexico Fellaheen," "The Railroad Earth," "Slobs of the Kitchen
      Sea," "New York Scenes," "Alone on a Mountaintop," "Big Trip to
      Europe," and "The Vanishing American Hobo.")
* *Old Angel Midnight.* London: Midnight Press, 1985. (An earlier edition
      contains only forty-nine of the complete sixty-seven strophes—Lon-
      don: Booklegger/Albion, n.d.)
* *Satori in Paris.* New York: Grove Press, 1966.
* *The Scripture of the Golden Eternity.* New York: Totem Press, 1960.

4. Poetry
  Heaven & Other Poems. Bolinas, Calif.: Grey Fox Press, 1977. (Contains
      also two brief autobiographical sketches written in 1957 and 1959
      and ten letters to Donald Allen written between 1957 and 1962.)
  Mexico City Blues. New York: Grove Press, 1959.
  Rimbaud. San Francisco: City Lights Books, 1960. (Broadside.)
  San Francisco Blues. London: Beat Books, 1983.
  Scattered Poems. San Francisco: City Lights Books, 1971.
  Trip Trap. With Albert Saijo and Lew Welch. Bolinas, Calif.: Grey Fox
      Press, 1973.

5. Film Narration
  Pull My Daisy. New York: Grove Press, 1961. (Transcription of overvoice
      narration delivered by Kerouac for Robert Frank's film, illustrated
      with stills from the film.)

6. Letters
  Dear Carolyn. California, Pa.: the unspeakable visions of the individual,
      1983. (Letters to Carolyn Cassady.)

SECONDARY SOURCES

  Only books and gatherings of shorter pieces are listed. For a detailed listing of American and international reviews of Kerouac's books and criticisms
of his life and work, see the bibliography by Robert J. Milewski listed be-
low. Biography and literary criticism are so intermingled in books about
Kerouac that it is impossible at this point to make any satisfactory distinction between them.

1. Bibliography
Charters, Ann. *A Bibliography of Works by Jack Kerouac (Jean-Louis Lebris de Kerouac), 1939–1975.* Rev. ed. New York: Phoenix Bookshop, 1975. (Original edition, including works through 1967, published by the same publisher in 1967.) The most complete listing available of Kerouac's books, contributions to magazines, recordings and other works, published in the United States and elsewhere in English and other languages, comprising the standard reference work on the author.

Milewski, Robert J. *Jack Kerouac: An Annotated Bibliography of Secondary Sources, 1944–1979).* The Scarecrow Author Bibliographies, no. 52, Metuchen, N. J.: Scarecrow Press, 1981. A keyed list of more than eight-hundred reviews in English and other languages of Kerouac's work and of general reviews and articles about his life and work, annotated with a description of the contents. The book is exhaustively indexed and contains several valuable appendixes including the last wills of Kerouac and his mother.

2. Books
Beaulieu, Victor-Lévy. *Jack Kerouac, Essai-Poulet.* Montreal: Editions du Jour, 1972. Reprinted in France as *Jack Kerouac* (Paris: Editions de L'Herne, 1973). Translated into English by Sheila Fischman as *Jack Kerouac: A Chicken-essay* (Toronto: Coach House Press, 1976). A French-Canadian novelist argues that Kerouac's work was greatly influenced by his Québécois heritage.

Bruccoli, Mary, ed. *Dictionary of Literary Biography. Documentary Series: An Illustrated Chronicle,* vol. 3, pp. 71–122. Detroit: Gale, 1983. A collection of biographical documents, including reviews and letters, arranged chronologically, and copiously illustrated. An invaluable source of reference materials.

Cassady, Carolyn. *Heart Beat: My Life with Jack & Neal.* Berkeley: Creative Arts Book Company, 1976. Reminiscences of the wife of Neal Cassady, original of Dean Moriarity in *On the Road* and Cody Pomeray of the Duluoz Legend. Material from the book provided the basis for the 1978 movie with the same title.

Challis, Chris. *Quest for Kerouac.* London: Faber & Faber, 1984. A remarkable account by a British university professor, who has written several academic theses on Kerouac, of his automobile trip across the United States, visiting places mentioned by Kerouac and interviewing his former associates, in an effort to evoke again the atmosphere of the United States in the 1950s during Kerouac's days on the road. No American has attempted such a project.

Charters, Ann, ed. *The Beats: Literary Bohemians in Postwar America. Dictionary of Literary Biography,* vol. 16. Detroit: Gale, 1984. The basic, indis-

pensable reference guide to the Beat Generation, edited by the foremost
Kerouac scholar. Contains articles by various writers on figures associated with and influenced by the Beat movement, as well as a general
chronology and appendices on Beat-oriented publications. The article
on Kerouac by George Dardess (1:278–303) is the most tearjerking example of the arguments of those who see Kerouac as a martyr to his
times and his associates.

————. *Kerouac: A Biography.* San Francisco: Straight Arrow, 1973. Although several later biographies have presented additional factual material, this pioneering work remains the one that best evokes Kerouac's
multifaceted personality and gives a sense of the ways in which he affected others.

————. *Scenes Along the Road: Photographs of the Desolation Angels/1944–1960.*
New York: Gotham Book Mart, 1970. A collection of photographs of
the Beats, including Kerouac, most of which had not appeared elsewhere.

Clark, Tom. *Jack Kerouac.* San Diego: Harcourt Brace Jovanovich, 1984.
The most up-to-date, concise, and carefully dated of the Kerouac biographies, with a profusion of illustrations. Must be used with care, however, in establishing biographical details because of Clark's tendency to
treat the novels as reliable records of events.

Cook, Bruce. *The Beat Generation.* New York: Scribner's, 1971. A general
history of the events leading up to the San Francisco Renaissance, with
special emphasis on the history of Kerouac's novels as the works that
publicized the Beat and influenced subsequent countercultural writers.

Feied, Frederick. *No Pie in the Sky: The Hobo as American Cultural Hero in
the Works of Jack London, John Dos Passos, and Jack Kerouac.* New York:
Citadel Press, 1964. Places Kerouac's work, especially *On the Road*, in
the context of an earlier American hobo tradition, but sees his characters
as taking to the road in social protest not from economic necessity.

Gaffié, Luc. *Jack Kerouac: The New Picaroon.* New York: Postillion Press,
1977. An examination of the elements of the picaresque tradition in
Kerouac's fiction.

Gifford, Barry. *Kerouac's Town.* Expanded rev. ed. Berkeley: Creative Arts
Book Co., 1977. (Originally published in 1973). Part 1 is an account
of a trip to Lowell on the second anniversary of Kerouac's death in
1971; Part 2 reports an interview with Kerouac's widow, Stella, in St.
Petersburg, Florida.

————. and **Lee, Lawrence.** *Jack's Book: An Oral Biography of Jack Kerouac.*
New York: St. Martin's Press, 1978. A biography composed principally
of quoted statements by those who had known Kerouac, tied together
with a running narrative by the editor/authors. The telling takes longer
than would a straightforward narrative, but the variety of styles keeps

the account exciting. Also contains as an appendix the best "Character Key to the Duluoz Legend" so far published, identifying the original of Kerouac's figures.

Ginsberg, Allen. *The Visions of the Great Rememberer.* Amherst, Mass.: Mulch Press, 1974. A memoir that picks up where Ginsberg's introduction to the 1972 edition of *Visions of Cody* leaves off. Includes letters from Neal Cassady and drawings by Basil King.

———— and **Cassady, Neal.** *As Ever: The Collected Correspondence of Allen Ginsberg and Neal Cassady.* Edited by Barry Gifford. Berkeley: Creative Arts Book Co., 1977. These letters from the 1940s to the 1960s contain frequent references to Kerouac.

Hipkiss, Robert A. *Jack Kerouac: Prophet of the New Romanticism.* Lawrence: Regents Press of Kansas, 1976. Compares Kerouac with Ken Kesey, John Knowles, James Purdy, and J. D. Salinger as promulgators of a new Romantic movement in American fiction, a position that has failed to win many adherents.

Holmes, John Clellon. *Nothing More to Declare.* New York: Dutton, 1967. This autobiography of the first writer to use Kerouac as a figure in one of his own novels traces their long relationship beginning in New York in the 1940s and the development of the Beat philosophy.

————. *Visitor: Jack Kerouac in Old Saybrook.* California, Pa.: the unspeakable visions of the individual, 1981. A beautifully produced, limited edition pamphlet, describing Kerouac's last sad visit to Holmes's Connecticut home.

————. *Gone in October: Last Reflections on Jack Kerouac.* Halley, Idaho: Limberlost Press, 1985. Four essays and a poem. The title piece describes Kerouac's funeral.

Huebel, Harry R. *Jack Kerouac.* Western Writers Series, No. 39. Boise, Idaho: Boise University Press, 1979. Part of a continuing pamphlet series presenting brief introductions to Western American writers, discussing Kerouac's contributions to the literature of California.

Hunt, Tim. *Kerouac's Crooked Road: Development of a Fiction.* Hamden, Conn.: Archon Books, 1981. The best critical study so far on any part of Kerouac's writings, this book concentrates on the development of the work that finally became *Visions of Cody*, which Kerouac regarded as his masterpiece, through four earlier versions, including the published text of *On the Road.* Traces the relationship also of the book to the American tradition of Melville and Mark Twain.

Jarvis, Charles E. *Visions of Kerouac.* Lowell, Mass.: Ithaca Press, 1973. A unique account by a close friend from Kerouac's home town of Lowell, Massachusetts, of the novelist's growing up and his home town associations. A somewhat naive account of Kerouac's life and works, but invaluable for its firsthand information.

Johnson, Joyce. *Minor Characters.* Boston: Houghton Mifflin, 1983. An intimate account of life with Kerouac during his last years in New York by the woman who then played one of the largest roles in his life.

McDarrah, Fred. *Kerouac and Friends: A Beat Generation Album.* New York: Morrow, 1984. A collection of 190 photographs by the famous portrayer of Greenwich Village life, accompanied by articles on the Beats.

McNally, Dennis. *Desolate Angel: Jack Kerouac, the Beats, and America.* New York: Random House, 1979. A pretentious effort to place the life of Kerouac and his associates against a background of the major events in American life from the 1930s to the 1960s, although Kerouac took little interest in most of the political or social developments.

Montgomery, John. *Kerouac West Coast: A Bohemian Pilot, Detailed Navigational Instructions.* Palo Alto, Calif.: Fels & Firn, 1976. An expansion of an earlier memoir that contains a wildly disorganized but valuable account of Kerouac's activities on the West Coast by a friend who is the original of Henry Morley in *The Dharma Bums.*

Nicosia, Gerald. *Memory Babe: A Critical Biography of Jack Kerouac.* New York: Grove Press, 1983. The most detailed biography of Kerouac to appear so far. (Nothing has been heard of an "official" biography by Aaron Latham, commissioned by Kerouac's agent, since the early 1970s). Nicosia's book contains a wealth of material from interviews and specific factual data missing from earlier accounts, but it is padded out with long uncritical panegyrics on Kerouac's writings.

Saroyan, Aram. *Genesis Angels: The Saga of Lew Welch and the Beat Generation.* New York: Morrow, 1979. Although primarily about Lew Welch (the model for Dave Wain in *Big Sur*), this biography by William Saroyan's son includes a great deal of material about Kerouac.

Tytell, John. *Naked Angels: The Lives and Literature of the Beat Generation.* New York: McGraw-Hill, 1976. Despite its sweeping title, the book is a biographical and critical study of Jack Kerouac, Allen Ginsberg, and William Burroughs.

Walsh, Joy. *Jack Kerouac: Statement in Brown.* Clarence Center, N.Y.: Textile Bridge Press, 1984. Nine essays on Kerouac and his work by the editor of *Moody Street Irregulars.*

3. Symposia devoted to Jack Kerouac and the Beats.

Bretagnes: Revue Littéraire et Politique Trimestrielle, No. 4 (1976). Edited by Paol Keineg. Half of this issue is devoted to articles on Kerouac by the editor and four other French scholars, letters, and a bibliography.

Burroughs, William S.; Kerouac, Jack; and **Pélieu, Claude.** *Jack Kerouac.* Paris: L'Herne, 1971. A memorial miscellany containing some notes by Kerouac, several pieces by the other editors, an elegy by Allen Ginsberg, with photographs and illustrations.

Donaldson, Scott, ed. *On the Road: Text and Criticism.* The Viking Critical Library. New York: Penguin Books, 1979. One of the most useful volumes for the study of Kerouac, containing a reset and corrected text of the novel and a number of important critical articles, as well as statements by the author.

Horemans, Rudi, ed. *Beat Indeed!* Antwerp, Belgium: EXA Publishers, 1985. An extremely useful collection of materials in English intended for European audiences, containing a variety of biographical and critical essays and the text of Arthur Knight's three-act play *King of the Beatniks,* based on Kerouac's last years.

Knight, Arthur and Glee, eds. *The Beat Book. the unspeakable visions of the individual,* vol. 4. California, Pa.: 1974. A gathering of material, mostly previously unpublished, about Kerouac and other Beats, including letters and photographs.

Knight, Arthur and Kit. *the unspeakable visions of the individual.* California, Pa.: various dates. Individual titles are: *The Beat Diary,* Vol. 5 (1977); *The Beat Journey,* Vol. 8 (1978); *Beat Angels,* Vol. 12 (1982); *The Beat Road,* Vol. 14 (1984). A unique and invaluable series of compilations of mostly previously unpublished writings, letters, and memoirs by and about Jack Kerouac and the other principal members of the Beat movement, profusely illustrated with photographs and drawings and reports of meetings devoted to Kerouac and the Beats.

Krim, Seymour. *The Beats.* Greenwich, Conn.: Gold Medal Books, 1960. One of the earliest compilations of materials about the Beats by a New York reporter who had observed their rise and the controversy it had generated.

Montgomery, John. *The Kerouac We Knew: Unposed Portraits, Action Shots.* Kentfield, Calif.: Fels & Firn, 1982. Six new essays and biographical notes honoring the Naropa Conference held in Boulder, Colorado, in July 1982 to celebrate the twenty-fifth anniversary of the publication of *On the Road.*

Parkinson, Thomas. *A Casebook on the Beat.* New York: Crowell, 1961. The first serious academic recognition of the Beats, this source book of a then popular type by a distinguished professor of English at the University of California-Berkeley who had followed the San Francisco Renaissance with sympathetic interest, provides now classic examples of the Beats' writings along with the most important sympathetic and condemnatory early criticisms of the movement.

Review of Contemporary Fiction 3, no. 2 (Summer, 1983). Edited by John O'Brien. This issue, devoted to Jack Kerouac and Robert Pinget, contains a selection of previously unpublished essays examining most facets of Kerouac's work.

Soundings/East 2, no. 2 (1979). This "Kerouac Issue" is a transcription of a symposium on Jack Kerouac at Salem State College, Massachusetts, in April 1973, directed by Professor Jay McHale. Contributors include Allen Ginsberg, Gregory Corso, John Clellon Holmes, and other friends and critics of Kerouac.

4. Journals

Kerouac Connection. Founded in January 1984 as the newsletter of the British Beat Brotherhood, this quarterly publication has become an independent journal devoted especially to news from Great Britain and the Continent and long, thoughtful reviews of books about Kerouac and the Beat Generation. Edited by Dave Moore, 19 Worthing Road, Patchway, Bristol, England BS12 5HY.

Moody Street Irregulars: A Jack Kerouac Newsletter. Founded in 1978 as a forum for Kerouac scholars and enthusiasts, this journal continues to appear about twice a year, featuring articles about Kerouac and other Beat writers and special issues on single subjects like the Naropa Conference. Edited by Joy Walsh, P. O. Box 157, Clarence Center, N.Y. 14032.

5. Films

Jack Kerouac's America. Produced and directed by John Antonelli, 1984. 90 minutes. This film by a former resident of Kerouac's hometown, Lowell, Massachusetts, dramatizes several passages from Kerouac's writings with Jack Coulter playing Kerouac. The 1982 Naropa Conference serves as a frame for the film with Carolyn Cassady and John Clellon Holmes as narrators. Premiered at the Mill Valley (California) Film Festival, 21 September 1984.

West Coast: Beat and Beyond. Videotape documentary produced and directed by Chris Felver with Gerald Nicosia. 60 minutes. First telecast on KQED in San Francisco in June 1984, it is narrated by Allen Ginsberg and features interviews with fifteen writers, including Lawrence Ferlinghetti, Ken Kesey, and Kerouac's daughter Jan Kerouac, discussing the San Francisco literary scene since the days of the 1950s Renaissance.

What Happened to Kerouac? Videotape documentary produced by Lewis MacAdams and Malcolm Hart. Metropolitan Films. 55 minutes. This film, which was first televised in Los Angeles in January 1985, features black-and-white clips of Kerouac's appearances on television shows, along with interviews of Ginsberg; Ferlinghetti; Carolyn Cassady, Kerouac's first wife, Edie Parker; and Jan Kerouac.

6. Plays about Kerouac

Duberman, Martin. *Visions of Kerouac, a Play.* Boston: Little, Brown, 1977. A biographical drama by a famous drama critic, who describes it as "a meditation on Kerouac's life," first performed in New York in December 1976.

Knight, Arthur. *King of the Beatniks.* Sudbury, Mass.: Water Row Press, 1985. A three-act play about a fictional "John Duhon," who is an alter ego of Jack Kerouac, and his relationships with his family and friends, first performed at the Shropshire Drama Festival in Donnington, England, in March 1985, but banned by the organizers of the Wrexham Festival in Wales.

Index